Classical Theories of Social Change

Classical Theories
of Social Change

LOUIS
SCHNEIDER

GENERAL LEARNING PRESS
250 James Street • Morristown, New Jersey 07960

Preface

In this short book, selected aspects of a number of older theories of social (and cultural) change are taken up. The time span covered runs roughly from the middle of the eighteenth century to the end of World War II, a period of almost two hundred years. The theories reviewed have their shortcomings. They are called "theories" by rather loose yet convenient usage, but it by no means follows that they are intellectually valueless. It may possibly be generous to apply the term "classical" to them, but they do constitute a significant background for modern sociological thought about change.

There is so much yet to be learned about social change that we can hardly afford to overlook any resources that may help us. It would be a mistake to regard the theories here reviewed as simply outmoded or as lacking all suggestiveness for those who are concerned to construct more powerful analyses of change than we now have. Whitehead's dictum that "a science which hesitates to forget its founders is lost" [Merton 1968, p. 1] is well balanced by the observation, "A science *ignorant* of its founders does not know how far it has travelled nor in what direction; it, too, is lost" [Gouldner, in Durkheim 1958, p. vi]. The theories we review are indeed "older" theories. It has just been implied that a certain significance still attaches to them. The combination of "age" and a continuing measure of significance is enough to justify the term "classical" in our title. We have also sought for items of some quality in the relevant older literature. A number of these are actually on the order of monuments of thought that may well always be worth returning to, whether or not they can directly stimulate contemporary reflection about change, and some justification of the term "classical" accordingly appears again.

The main aim in what follows is just to afford, by way of a selective survey, a good sense of what has been done in the past in the field reviewed. There is a strong concentration on the work of individual thinkers in sociology and there is some attention to anthropology. There has had to be a measure of arbitrariness in the choices made. A man like Oswald Spengler, whose *Decline of the West* [Spengler 1939] made a considerable stir after World War I, is barely referred to toward the end of the present essay. It must suffice to say that, exclusions being unavoidable, preference over Spengler was given to figures like the sociologist Pitirim A. Sorokin and the anthropologist Alfred L. Kroeber, who had interests somewhat like those of Spengler. The historian Arnold Toynbee, whose vast *Study of History* might well merit consideration in a longer piece than this one, could only be referred to incidentally and in regard to a single special, although significant, point in the text that follows.

Choice is also involved in that attention has been limited to theories of the so-called "macro" type. These theories generally reflect a concern with large-scale social systems or schemes and large-scale changes. The character and fortunes of entire societies or sets of societies, major changes within or about them, the actions of large social classes rather than of small groups—these things at least suggest the kinds of preoccupations one may expect of macro theorists. The theme of the evolution of societies (involving, say, transitions from the state of primitive hunters all the way to the so-called civilized condition) is a main one. It points of course to major structural changes. This particular macro theme of evolution will indeed take up much of our space.

Evolutionary theory will, appropriately enough, then, be the first subject considered. It is followed by a very short section on dualistic development theory, which is still dominated by evolutionary concerns, and by a section on cyclical theories of change. Evolutionary thought and cyclical thought have stimulated one another and are not necessarily in all respects incompatible with one another, although modern cyclical thought has some background of revolt against a too facile evolutionary optimism.

A penultimate section is entitled "Conflict, Reason, Religion, and Charisma: Karl Marx and Max Weber." Marx and Frederick Engels were hospitable to the evolutionary thought of a man like the anthropologist Lewis Henry Morgan, but of course Marx had his own distinctive way of discussing change and relating it closely to conflict. There is good reason to juxtapose Marx and Weber, the latter of whom was much influenced by the former even if a number of his ideas here most pertinent are quite different from the former's.

A final section consists of notes on technology and culture. It deals with some views of William F. Ogburn and Alfred L. Kroeber. In the further course of this preface, our concerns with the relations of technology and culture will be more fully referred to. Suffice it to say at this point that such an interest might well be anticipated in any case in a book that touches on some theories that are "materialistic" and on others that are "idealistic" in tone.

The reader should find it helpful that there are at least three large, integrating concerns, that the writer has pursued. One is a concern with what may be called dialectic. There is much about social life that has a flavor of paradox or dilemma. Sometimes failure, curiously, presages or somehow involves success—or success, failure. Strength may give rise to weakness, as when a show of brutal power arouses deep resentments in those over whom it is exercised and ultimately brings ruin upon the brutal power. A social system often gives the impression that it is well analyzed as a complex totality in which opposites are united and in which tensions and ambiguities are constantly present. Ideally, it might be argued, a system reference should always be included when we talk in dialectical terms. We tend to use the term "dialectic" here, however, in a somewhat casual way, yet in a way that will be sufficiently clear in particular cases as we refer to Adam Ferguson, Herbert Spencer, Pitirim Sorokin, and Karl Marx. It should be added that there is certainly nothing incompatible between a dialectical outlook as we conceive it and sustained thought about social structure or cultural phenomena. The concern with dialectic is sufficiently pervasive so that a sense of continuity or of holding to certain objects throughout should be supported by it.

A second concern that calls for mention and that will be stressed in more than one place is with the role that is assigned to human choice in social change. This concern will be particularly important in our discussions of Hobhouse and, again, of Marx.

There is a third concern that is taken up in the following pages that in a very general way also "pulls together" some of our materials. The concern here is at least to leave the reader with the persuasion that anything like a "proper" lining up or array or arrangement of what are roughly designated as technological and economic factors, on the one hand, and cultural factors, on the other, in analysis of major changes, is still unachieved in the classical theories. It is questionable if much progress has been made in the whole matter in postclassical theories [see, however, Parsons 1966, Ch. 2].

The dichotomy, technological-economic versus cultural, is of course over-simplified. Thus, technology is itself in a very evident sense a part of man's culture, a heritage handed down from one generation to another, and it may be profoundly shaped by cultural factors from outside technology. (But just how is it shaped by extra-technological factors?) Economic interests or economic structures may be deeply affected by religion. (But again, just how?) They are likely to be pervaded by, say, legal norms, which are as cultural as anything can be. Granted the excessive simplicity of our dichotomy and granted the influences to which we refer (as of religion on economic factors) and which are really quite obvious in a general way, it may yet be contended that a very large challenge to a theory of social change lies in "proper" or "correct" conceptions of the relations of the technological-economic and the cultural.

Technological and economic emphases will certainly

be found as the reader goes through the following, as will cultural emphases. Again, these must not be simplistically opposed. Nevertheless, as readers review, say, Marx on the one hand and Weber on the other, Ogburn on the one hand and Kroeber on the other, it is to be hoped that they will obtain a keener appreciation for the concern indicated—one keen enough to alert them even to current manifestations of this concern which we cannot take up.

Chronological order is closely followed, although it may not be as we switch from one large subject to another. Relevant thought beyond our time span is referred to when it seems likely to be especially helpful to do so. In a number of cases, where it seems important to indicate original dates of publication, these are given.

LOUIS SCHNEIDER

Contents

The Idea
of Social Evolution

Evolutionary thought was prominent in sociology and anthropology into the earlier part of the twentieth century. Although it lost popularity in these fields thereafter, it has had some revival lately. The classical theories of change strongly feature evolutionary thought.

One could not get complete agreement on what constitutes social or cultural evolution or even, perhaps, on what it meant for the classical theorists. Two ideas, however, those of adaptation and what may be called movement from homogeneity to heterogeneity, have been important elements of the general conception of evolution. While a conclusive definition of what evolution means or of what it meant to the older theorists cannot be offered, we can still learn some highly pertinent things by attending to these two notions.

Adaptation

Adaptation refers to adjustment to environmental conditions. Enhanced adaptation means better or more effective coping with such conditions. Technology at once calls for consideration. When human beings changed from the use of stone to the use of metal to make weapons and utensils, there was a considerable increase in technical efficiency and flexibility. The changeover from stone to metal represented a *major* adaptive enhancement in human history and therefore may be said to have had evolutionary significance. Obviously, however, it would be absurd to regard every small improvement in the construction of a knife or the making of an ax as an "evolutionary" change.

Adaptation need not refer to adjustment to the physical environment alone. It may refer to adjustment to the environment of surrounding societies. In case of recourse to war, plainly, a society with a technology that is more advanced than that of other societies, in spheres pertinent to the effective waging of war, will be better "adapted" than the others.

There is a kind of change or enhanced adaptation in the occupational area that is closely related to change or enhanced adaptation in the technological area. A society may go from a "stage" of hunting and fishing to agriculture. As this movement occurs, new tools and instruments appear, and there is better all-round coping with the physical environment, which is now likely to "yield" much more than it did before. Again, this is a *major* occupational shift and may be considered to have evolutionary significance.

It is evident that there is a cognitive factor—a factor of

sheer knowledge—involved in technology. In particular cases it may not be highly refined knowledge. It may not be highly systematic knowledge. But it is knowledge nevertheless, even if it involves no more than knowing how to make a bow and arrow or a so-called atlatl (spearthrower). At the same time, the cognitive element, the knowledge factor, can reach well beyond technology as such. There was much stress on cognitive progress in classical evolutionary theory.

One such line of theory postulated a general movement from magic to religion to science. This sort of movement was envisaged, for example, by the famed anthropologist James G. Frazer, who argued that there was a broad shift in the history of mankind from an Age of Magic to an Age of Religion, and, finally, to an Age of Science. Everywhere, Frazer surmises, "an Age of Religion has . . . been preceded by an Age of Magic" [1958, p. 65]. But for Frazer, magic, religion, and science are all modes of approaching the world that have heavy cognitive components. For him, magic is essentially a pseudoscience that rests on illusion about the world of reality. Religion involves practice as well as belief, but Frazer insists that "belief clearly comes first" [1958, p. 58], and the cognitive element in religion is evidently of great importance for him. One need hardly bother to stress the cognitive element in science, since it is so evident.

There is more than one difficulty with this sort of developmental scheme. An important question is whether magic and religion belong in the same historical or evolutionary *series* with science. For example, it might well be argued that the primary significance of magic is not cognitive at all. Magic may be interpreted as a manipulative effort at control that merely throws up a kind of cognitive screen, while its real character is that of an essentially noncognitive thrust toward deeply cherished human goals that man often cannot achieve. Its motto would appear to be, "Let me have! Let me have good things and avoid evil ones!" "Gimme!" rather than "Let me know! Let me understand!" So, too, in the case of religion, many of its students today regard it as having to do with "life," with "existence," with teaching "how to live" in the light of spiritual inspiration, while the cognitive element in it, although unquestionably present and significant, is not of overwhelming importance. The cognitive element in science may then seem to be more salient than in magic or religion. Perhaps science is best put in a series with philosophical or technological thought. Or it might be best to recognize that one should have a *number* of developmental series in order to do justice to a complex historical reality.

If we take the magic-to-religion-to-science notion literally or in very extreme form, the question arises of how man ever survived to the present day. While fooling with ultimately ineffective devices based on the pseudoscience of magic, how did he manage to live? Was there no technology along with magic? Were there no elements of science, however rudimentary, in the Age of Magic?

We need not strain too much over the whole matter. Magic, religion, and science have in fact been much intermixed. Even today, there may well be elements of magic mingled with science in its various forms. And, when all criticisms have been made, Frazer did sense correctly a point that is after all rather plain. In a broad, general way human history does reveal a certain cognitive progress. True, progress is progress *by certain criteria*. But in terms, for example, of scientific achievement, ancient Egypt and Mesopotamia simply cannot be compared with the modern West. Babylonian astronomy is childish compared with astronomy today. The development of logic in classical Greece, with which Aristotle is heavily identified, represented the development of an analytical tool never before equalled and subsequently refined and improved.

As we shall see, Auguste Comte, the French thinker who is sometimes called "the founder of sociology," had an essentially cognitive-evolutionary view of history that raises problems that will remind us of Frazer. But, in any case, one can easily argue for a kind of cognitive progress in the general course of human history that involves fields of knowledge beyond technology. Here again we have increased adaptation or adaptiveness, most obviously where enhancement or improvement of science is concerned. (In its fuller effects, science may involve us in new problems of "adaptation" that can strike us as most difficult or unfortunate, but that is really quite another matter.)

Homogeneity and Heterogeneity

The movement from homogeneity to heterogeneity also often clearly involves enhanced adaptation, but the notion of adaptation is not sufficient to cover it. The terms homogeneity and heterogeneity are taken directly from Herbert Spencer, the great nineteenth-century theorist of evolution. Spencer emphasized, as basic to evolution in the broadest sense, transition from states of indefinite, incoherent homogeneity to states of definite, coherent heterogeneity.

One significant formulation of Spencer's basic view runs, "Evolution is an integration of matter and concomitant dissipation of notion, during which the matter passes from an indefinite, incoherent homogeneity to a definite, coherent heterogeneity; and during which the retained motion undergoes a parallel transformation" [Spencer 1958, p. 394]. In the same book from which this is drawn, Spencer gives a simpler version of his basic idea: "Evolution is a change from an indefinite, incoherent homogeneity to a definite, coherent heterogeneity through continuous differentiations and integrations" [1958, p 554]. (A delightful "translation" of Spencer on evolution with which he himself was familiar, goes, "Evolution is a change from a nohowish, untalkaboutable all-alikeness, to a somehowish and in general talkaboutable not-all-alikeness, by continuous somethingelseifications and stick-togetherations" [Spencer 1958, p. 554].)

We can use the simpler definition and spare ourselves some unnecessary difficulties. The "indefiniteness" of "indefinite, incoherent homogeneity" refers to lack of sharpness of outline or structure. Incoherence means a state of "not sticking together." Homogeneity refers to sameness of composition throughout. For our limited purposes, we may say that, in Spencer's view, "unevolved" organisms, for example, would be organisms whose "parts" lack sharpness of outline or are only rudimentarily differentiated. Such organisms would be loosely organized. The parts of such organisms, if they were separated by cutting, might sustain independent life. By analogy, the "parts" or "structures" of a society may also show relatively little sharpness of outline, low differentiation, and high capacity to sustain independent life when separated. When sharpness of outline, clear differentiation, and tighter cohesion have occurred, both organisms and societies would be more "evolved." They would show definite, coherent heterogeneity. Processes of integration would bring about the cohesion. These processes *must not* be overlooked.

Structural differentiation and integration are crucial in the Spencerian notion of movement from homogeneity to heterogeneity. Since Spencer anticipated contemporary discussion of evolution, as by Talcott Parsons [1966], we may borrow a good deal from Parsons to exemplify Spencer's conception of differentiation and integration, while realizing that the ideas to be noted are really rather close to Spencer's. In other words, we borrow from the *contemporary* Parsons merely in order to clarify *older* social-evolutionary notions. (In this case, the danger of reading present thought into the past is not very great.) [For an interesting if exaggerated recent criticism of neo-evolutionary thought, see Smith 1973.]

One of the notable processes of structural differentiation that occurred as England moved into its eighteenth-century Industrial Revolution had to do with the separation of economic activity from the kin group or family. The old *fusion* of kin group and family was broken up as the kinship-economic production structure gave way to *two* distinctive structures—a kin structure now relatively emptied of economic production activity, and an economic structure of factories and, one may also say, offices. In a more "evolved" state of society, the kin group or family is "housed" in a different structure from that which "houses" the newly emergent factory or office. "Parts" of society are to this extent now more sharply outlined, more clearly differentiated. They are more "definite." Heterogeneity has been introduced with the differentiation.

At the same time, however, independent existence for

kin-family on the one hand and factory-office on the other is quite impossible. The structurally differentiated "parts" are highly interdependent. They "stick together," which is, of course, the precise meaning of "cohere."

Moreover, the parts are "integrated," or at least (to put the matter more cautiously) "problems" of integration arise. Thus, for example, the worker ordinarily wants to be able to get back to his family after a day at the factory or office. This requires a social-ecological integration, an organization of the factor of distance so that the worker can indeed get home—and more or less conveniently return to work the next day. Family and work are thus integrated through appropriate transportation schemes, time schedules, and so on.

Again, there are new problems of integration centering around authority. When people did a great deal of their work within kin groups, there was a kind of "natural" integration of work activities and an enforcement of work discipline through the traditional authority of figures such as the father or male kin-group head. With work transferred from cottage (or farm) to factory or office, the "natural" kin authority can no longer work in the same way. Workers have to be organized on the basis of new authority; work discipline has to be set up in new ways.

New industrialists and managerial groups did not always find it easy to solve the problems of pulling together ("integrating") their labor forces and inducing disciplined behavior. Some of the difficulties they faced are indicated by Thompson [1964] and by Smelser, who refers pertinently to "improving the moral habits of the working populace in the matter of orderliness, punctuality, regularity, and temperance" [1959, p. 106]. This is not to imply that England's new factory workers in the eighteenth century had to be "saved" by benevolent masters and managers, but rather that problems were created by the mere absence, in factory and office, of the traditional authority of the head of a kin group. The kin group was also a producing economic unit whose work the head could oversee and pull together. These problems, of course, were not peculiar to industrializing England.

The whole development just reviewed meant a great increase in economic adaptiveness, effectiveness, and productivity. Without doubt it also involved human costs. Was there also increased adaptiveness for the kin group or family? Was the changed kin or family structure, with fewer functions to perform, better able to perform those functions it retained? This is difficult to answer, and even if the answer is affirmative, it is inconclusively so.

There are structural differentiations and integrations that do not bear on the economic sphere, in the case of which, generally speaking, the criteria of adaptation or adaptiveness or "adaptive upgrading" might become quite complex and where we might hesitate as to whether a clear verdict of "upgrading" should be allowed. But this must not be allowed to divert us. It is sufficient to note two things: (1) structural differentiation and integration *can* indeed be accompanied by enhanced adaptiveness; (2) such differentiation and integration do in fact extend far beyond economic spheres or anything very immediately pertinent to such spheres. Note, for example, the following statement by Spencer.

There has to be . . . described the evolution of the ecclesiastical structures and functions. Commencing with these as scarcely distinguished from the political structures and functions, their divergent developments must be traced.

How the share of ecclesiastical agencies in political actions becomes gradually less; how, reciprocally, political agencies play a decreasing part in ecclesiastical actions, are phenomena to be set forth. How the internal organization of the priesthood, differentiating and integrating as the society grows, stands related in type to the co-existing organizations, political and other; and how changes of structure in it are connected with changes in structure in them; are also subjects to be dealt with [Spencer 1899, I:438–439].

It may be mentioned here that the notion of movement from homogeneity to heterogeneity (involving differentiation and integration) can be applied also to more strictly cultural forms, to a field, for instance, such as art. Spencer himself discerned some fascinating problems in this cultural sphere, but again we refer to a matter that can only be mentioned in passing [but see Munro 1963].

Evolution and Progress

It will be clear by now that evolution has some connection with progress. But caution about such connections is also needed. Progress—"forward movement"—in the evolutionary course is not always obvious or beyond argument. Leonard T. Hobhouse, who will be discussed in some detail later, deserves preliminary mention in this context. Hobhouse was one of the more prominent sociologists who worked into the earlier twentieth century with a rather sophisticated version of evolutionary theory. He argued in a late book [1924, p. 78] that a community evolves or "develops" as it advances in scale, efficiency, freedom, and neutrality. Scale means simply size. One need not quarrel with this. (Advancing technological and occupational development are very likely to enhance scale or size.) Efficiency, as Hobhouse thought of it, has aspects that are not strictly reducible to technology or control over nature. It is connected with processes of differentiation, division of labor, and specialization. There is nothing to quarrel about here either, and we may readily concede to Hobhouse that along with the processes just referred to there goes some measure of "integration through organized control" [1924, p. 32]. But what about "personal freedom"?

Hobhouse contended that in the "higher," more evolved communities there is also greater personal freedom than in the "lower." He believed that a kind of common life supervenes that enhances the individual personality. It is not that we doubt that Hobhouse had a point even here. But "personal freedom" becomes hedged with some extremely difficult questions, and there is room for considerable controversy about its scope and significance as one moves from one kind of "stage" of society to another.

It is foolish or illusory to think of evolution as implying progress in any overall sense or to think that it must lead to utter human bliss. From a vastly advanced technology people may look back to a more primitive one under which they might conceivably have been happier or less miserable. It now seems almost incredible that Spencer could once write that ". . . evolution can end only in the establishment of the greatest perfection and the most complete happiness" [1958, originally 1862, p. 511]. We must be careful, however, not to attribute to him a naïveté about evolution of which he was not guilty. But it is noteworthy that, at the end of the third volume of his major work on *Principles of Sociology*, he adheres not to "an absolute optimism but to a relative optimism." He acknowledges here that ". . . the cosmic process brings about retrogression as well as progression, where the conditions favor it." He also avers that ". . . evolution does not imply a latent tendency to improve, everywhere in operation" and that "there is no uniform ascent from lower to higher" [1899, III:609]. At least a touch, if not of black then of gray, thus creeps into the evolutionary white.

Our own understanding of evolutionary social theory, particularly in its classical forms, should enlarge and deepen as we go on. We shall be considering matters not thus far covered or not thus far sufficiently discussed. But the points already covered may provide a helpful background as we go on to present pertinent views that stretch from the days of Adam Smith (d. 1790) to those of Hobhouse (d. 1924) and Émile Durkheim (d. 1917).

We proceed, then, to deal in the present framework of evolutionary thought with Adam Smith and two of his fellow Scots, Adam Ferguson and John Millar, all three of whom were notable evolutionary social scientists. After considering these men, we turn to Auguste Comte, who gave sociology its name, and then consider the anthropologist Lewis Henry Morgan, Spencer again in more detail, Hobhouse, and finally Durkheim under a separate heading, although the work of his which we touch upon is still very much in the evolutionary spirit.

Scottish Thought on Evolutionary Change: Adam Smith, Adam Ferguson, and John Millar

Smith on the Developmental Sequence of Society

Adam Smith (1723–1790) was a professor of moral philosophy at the University of Glasgow. Because of the great impact of his work *The Wealth of Nations,* he is often referred to as the "father of modern economics." He was also an able sociologist at a time when that word was not yet in use.

There is a little that is pertinent for us in Smith's early *Lectures on Justice, Police, Revenue and Arms* [1896]. Hunters and fishermen are to be found in a first "period of society." Smith evidently considered it appropriate to apply the term "savages" to them. Their period is followed by one of shepherds. After the shepherd period there is one of farming, and then there is a commercial period. The scheme here is extremely simple, hardly a scheme at all, for Smith's relevant statements are very spare [1896, pp. 14-15, 18, 20, 53, 107]. There is the quite explicit affirmation, "The four stages of society are hunting, pasturage, farming, and commerce" [1896, p. 107], Smith's lectures abound in phrases, such as "the infancy of society," "the beginnings of society," "in rude ages," "in rude and barbarous periods," that are quite conformable with the notion of an evolution of society.

The developmental sequence suggested in Smith's much more important work, *The Wealth of Nations* [1937, originally 1776], is very similar to that presented in the *Lectures*. Smith refers in the more important work to ". . . nations of hunters, the lowest and rudest state of society, such as we find it among the native tribes of North America," where "every man is a warrior as well as a hunter" [1937, p. 653]. Then there is reference to ". . . nations of shepherds, a more advanced state of society, such as we find it among the Tartars and Arabs" [p. 653]. Smith also refers later to "the age of shepherds" as the second period of society." When at a much later point [p. 735] he refers to ". . . the barbarous societies of hunters, of shepherds, and even of husbandmen in that rude state of husbandry which precedes the improvement of manufacturers, and the extension of foreign commerce," we note that "barbarous" is now applied to hunters, who were called "savages" in the *Lectures*. But the presentation is still much the same as it was before. Piecing together relevant statements in *The Wealth of Nations*, one comes out with this sequence (relating, be it noted, to salient occupations):

- Hunters
- Shepherds

- Primitive agriculturalists

- Advanced agriculturalists

- "Civilized" men (with "improved" manufactures and engaged in foreign commerce)

This sort of sequence has changed remarkably little since Smith's day. Nearly a century and a half after Smith's work, Hobhouse, Wheeler, and Ginsberg [1965, originally 1915] set out a sequential scheme of eight stages, namely, those of Lower Hunters, Higher Hunters, and Dependent Hunters, followed by a first Agricultural Stage, then by a first Pastoral Stage, further followed by a second Agricultural Stage, a second Pastoral Stage, and a third Agricultural Stage. Hobhouse, Wheeler, and Ginsberg stop short of "civilization." Nearly a full two centuries after Smith, the Lenskis' unusual textbook in macrosociology [Lenski & Lenski 1974] presents a rather similar scheme in which they begin with hunting and gathering societies, proceed to "horticultural" societies, go then to agricultural societies, stop to consider "specialized societal types" (fishing, herding, and maritime societies), and then go on finally to "industrial and industrializing societies."

Perhaps it is inevitable that this sort of sequencing should not have changed much in 200 years. A certain general occupational typing is readily suggested by the character of the data one deals with, and the variations one can introduce clearly cannot be very large if one is committed to categories such as "hunters" or "agriculturalists."

At this point we must make explicit a matter that cannot be avoided in discussion of stages of development.

Smith apparently intended to present what one may call a holistic scheme of social evolution. He did not pretend to trace, in one *particular* society after another, a sequence from hunting to shepherding to primitive agriculture, and so on. His sequence rather appears to be derived from a broad consideration of human history as a *whole*—hence, of course, our word "holistic." (This in turn points to some important questions about the work of the classical evolutionists that we shall have to consider with some care when we take up the work of Lewis Henry Morgan.) In broad, sweeping historical terms, when we "pick" our stages or periods from different societies or different historical series, some such sequence as Smith postulated can certainly be justified.

This does not mean that Smith would have rejected out of hand the notion that there are *some* similarities in sequences from the case of one particular society to another. But he does not imply any unqualified necessity that "all societies must go through the same stages." In *The Wealth of Nations* [Book III, chapter IV], discussing commerce and town development, Smith argues that in most of Europe commerce and urban manufacture have *caused* "the improvement and cultivation of the country" rather than having been the *effect* of rural improvement. For him, this is contrary to "the natural course of things." For, according to the natural course of things, ". . . the greater part of the capital of every growing society is, first, directed to agriculture, afterwards to manufacture, and last of all to foreign commerce" [1937, p. 360]. Smith soon added to this that ". . . though this natural order of things must have taken place in some degree in every such society, it has, in all the modern states of Europe been, in many respects, entirely inverted" [p. 360]. The impression of flexibility in Smith's developmental or evolutionary scheme is bound to be a strong one for any careful reader of his work.

Ferguson on Development and Dialectic

Adam Ferguson (1723–1816) was, like Smith, a professor of moral philosophy; however, Ferguson was affiliated with the University of Edinburgh. His thought anticipates a surprising amount of modern sociological work.

Ferguson argued that "the history of mankind in their rudest state" may be considered under two heads—first, "that of the savage who is not yet acquainted with property"; second, "that of the barbarian," to whom property is, "although not ascertained by laws," yet a principal object of his wishes [1966, originally 1767, p. 82]. Men definitely go from a savage state to a barbarous one, and "the most remarkable races of men have been rude before they were polished," but Ferguson adds, very interestingly, that "they have in some cases returned to barbarism again" [p. 109]. Savagery and barbarism are followed by a state of civility. In this, the arts develop, economic organization becomes more complex, class lines are more strongly drawn than before, commerce becomes important, and there is often a decline of inner solidarity in a nation—accompanied or marked by a loosening of bonds of affection [see Lehmann 1930, pp. 81–85].

The savagery-barbarism-civility (or civilization) sequence (not clearly and simply an outcome of occupational typing) is also one that was endlessly repeated in subsequent work. Thus, for example, the full title of

Lewis Henry Morgan's important volume, *Ancient Society*, was *Ancient Society or Researches in the Lines of Human Progress from Savagery through Barbarism to Civilization* [1964, originally 1877].

Ferguson advances views that suggest "degenerative" or corrupting effects of wealth and an outcome of despotism in the course of social and political developments. He does not seem to insist, however, on an inevitable decline of societies, even if one also takes into account his large historical work, *The History of the Progress and Termination of the Roman Republic* [1825, originally 1783]. In his view, a prime fact of the Roman historical scene was that "the republican form of government was exchanged for despotism" [1825, p. 2]. It is highly characteristic for Ferguson to observe that, in the first century B.C. in Rome, men became ". . . glutted with material prosperity; they thought that they were born to enjoy what their fathers had won, and saw not the use of those austere and arduous virtues by which the State had increased to its present greatness" [pp. 169–170].

Despite Ferguson's sharp eye for what he considered the degenerating effects of wealth and his notion of the likelihood of the decline of virtue under conditions of civilization, he still had a strong streak of voluntarism, that is, he believed man can will his own welfare and bring it about; his destiny is in his own hands. It is arguable whether Ferguson really held to a cyclical view of history, with always inevitable moral decay succeeded by new upturns (compare Forbes' "Introduction" to Ferguson [1966] with Lehmann [1930, pp. 81–85]).

In connection with his evolutionary concerns, Ferguson may reveal a dialectical bent. This bent is of considerable interest to us in any case, whether or not it appears in intimate connection with specifically evolutionary concerns, although in the writers whom we treat it frequently does. Ferguson's sense for the paradoxical in social change, his feeling for the intimate connection of failure and success, weakness and strength is brought out in a remarkable passage in his large-scale historical work on Rome.

The Romans, by the continual labours of seven centuries, had made their way from the Tiber to the Rhine and the Danube, through the territory of warlike hordes who opposed them, and over forests and rugged ways that were everywhere to be cleared at the expense of their labour and their blood: but the ways they had made to reach their enemies were now open, in their turns, for enemies to reach them. The ample resources which they had formed by their cultivation increased the temptation to invade them, and facilitated all the means of making war upon their country. By reducing the inhabitants of their provinces, in every part, to pacific subjects, they brought the defense of the empire to depend on a few professional soldiers who composed the legions [1825, p. 432]. (Ferguson writes this under the date U.C. 760, that is, it is an observation pertinent to Rome some 760 years after the presumed founding of the city in 753 B.C.)

". . . but the ways they had made to reach their enemies were now open, in their turns, for enemies to reach them." The successful enterprise of the Romans opens the road to their downfall or failure. "The ample resources which they had formed by their cultivation increased the temptation to invade them, and facilitated all the means of making war upon their country." The very triumphs of the Romans invited and prepared the way for their defeats. The dialectical bent of Ferguson is evident. This sort of bent can be extremely revealing in theories of social change. But it must *pay its way* by the most careful analyses we can present and the most rigorous checking of pertinent facts that we can manage. Otherwise, there is some danger of our being fooled by intriguing verbal formulas.

Millar on Historical Sociology

John Millar (1735–1801) is the third of the outstanding Scottish social scientists we are considering. Millar taught civil law at the University of Glasgow and did distinguished work in what today might be called historical sociology. He also entertained views that are interesting in the light of the idea of social evolution. There are three matters regarding which Millar deserves some comment in the present account.

First, he believed that a slow evolution of major human establishments or institutions had taken place over time. He inclined to the view that this slow evolution tends to give institutions a certain value or utility or functionality. The institutions incorporate, as it were, the experience and wisdom that have been gained in the long history of communities. Millar was trained as a lawyer and his major work is entitled *An Historical View of the English Government* [1803, originally 1787]. The law or the constitution, for him, clearly often embodies an accumulated wisdom, likely to transcend by far the wisdom of any particular person at any particular time. The law, one might say, is like a language into which numerous speakers and writers over the generations have poured their ingenuity.

Insofar as this view is present in Millar, he had a certain trust in evolutionary processes in society. He was suspicious of human meddling and looked with a jaundiced eye on the activities of those whom he called political "projectors" or regarded as makers of schemes. He tended not to attribute a tremendous amount of efficacy to human reason in bringing about useful, "functional" establishments or institutions. He had some reservations about future reliance on reason in achieving social utilities. He perceived a sort of tacit "reason" in the evolutionary process itself.

Although all this constitutes an important strain in Millar, we have sought to state it quite cautiously. Millar could *also* be critical of human institutions, the precipitates of evolutionary processes, and he had a markedly nonconservative side [Schneider 1971–72]. He could at times see institutions as incorporating foolishness or even absurdity. The first strain that we have noted remained very important in Millar, even if it is in tension with other elements of his intellectual makeup.

Second, we note that for Millar, as for many eighteenth-century thinkers (among them Millar's prominent fellow social scientists, Smith and Ferguson) it is a matter for stress that in the course of social evolution man's social actions often bring results that were never intended or anticipated. Constitutions may develop that in time represent imposing structures so neatly organized and integrated that we come easily to think that they must have been deliberate human creations.

Millar refers to the Anglo-Saxon government as one ". . . in which we may discover so much order and regularity, such a variety of regulations, nicely adjusted to one another" and so much human usefulness that ". . . it is natural to suppose that the whole has originated in much contrivance and forethought; and is the result of deep-laid schemes of policy" [1803, I:375]. But Millar goes on to argue very persuasively that immensely useful constitutions have been built piecemeal by human actors who never had in mind what those constitutions in their totality would finally amount to and what large functions they would in the end subserve. Particles of action, so to say, build up over time into mighty structures that, once again, incorporate wisdom and advance human welfare. (Of course, in principle, unanticipated or unintended effects of social action might at times work out to human detriment and not to human advantage.) Here we see that if there is indeed "reason" in the evolutionary process, it is a "reason" that no human mind ever encompassed in its totality, but a reason that got built into human establishments bit by bit via the contribution of many minds working to an end they neither contemplated nor foresaw.

Third, and finally, we note that, in discussing the history of the English government, Millar draws parallels with other countries. Thus, he sees parallel lines in the social evolution of England and Germany. Like developments occur in different societies on the basis of similar sociocultural backgrounds and on the basis of the need to meet similar conditions or situations. Describing more or less simultaneous change both in England and all the Western European kingdoms, Millar observes that this "appears to have proceeded from the natural course of the feudal governments" [1803, II:19]. But it would be erroneous to infer that Millar's conception of social evolution implies a rigidly similar sequence of stages for all societies. He was far too well informed historically, far too aware of the empirical realities of divergence to be partial to such rigidity.

It must not be supposed that the Scots stand intellectually isolated in relation to the further development of sociology or economics. Thus, Adam Smith and Adam Ferguson were known to Karl Marx and there is reason to claim some knowledge of Scottish social science for Herbert Spencer. (It is well known, moreover, that Smith in particular influenced the further development of economics. However, it is by no means a major objective of this essay to trace historical lines of the influence of thought. Our interest is not so much in following *intellectual history* as in presenting *thought from the past*. Our next section is in line with a simple chronological sequence. The Scottish movement in social thought that we have considered through three of its most important representatives had attained most of what it was due to attain by the end of the eighteenth century. The Frenchman, Auguste Comte, was born near the end of the same century. There is certainly some justification for taking Comte as the next considerable figure after the Scots in the dawning modern discipline of sociology. It is appropriate, then, to go on to Comte at this juncture.

The Movement of History: Auguste Comte

Engaged with both philosophy and sociology, Auguste Comte (1798–1857) is sure to be long remembered, at the very least for having given the latter discipline its name. Comte believed he discerned a great movement in human history from theological to metaphysical to positive or scientific modes of thought.

Theological philosophy comes first in human development. Man attributes to external phenomena a life like his own, and then he conceives of supernatural agents that he believes amenable to his desires. "Fetichism" is Comte's word for the very primitive philosophy or idea-system, under the sway of which there is a great tendency for things to be personified, endowed with passion, and deified [Comte 1853, II:190]. Comte thinks that fetichism in time gives way to star worship (astrolatry) and finally to full-scale polytheism. But this is all still within the "theological" stage, which is above all marked by a mode of thought or a way of knowing, just as are the two great later stages—metaphysical and positive. Comte's stress is heavily cognitive.

Comte's analysis of the metaphysical stage is in its way quite modern (although he hardly disposes of all "metaphysical" questions in the broadest sense of that term). Comte understood that one can make great play with ambitious words suggesting much knowledge where there is actually much ignorance. The word "phlogiston" is a familiar example of such words. Phlogiston was thought of as a principle of combustibility inhering in substances that could be put on fire. Substances could accordingly be put on fire because they had something in them inherently capable of being put on fire. (This "metaphysical" bias of "phlogiston" is stressed despite whatever utility the concept may have had otherwise in the history of science up to a certain time.)

This kind of "metaphysical" ineptitude was devastatingly criticized by Comte. He was alert to the procedure of giving some phenomenon a name and then supposing one had discovered something significant about it by moving the name around and taking it as somehow explanatory of things. Comte had a healthy suspicion of such things as inherent principles and ghostly substances and "entities." A simplified summary of the supposed transition from the theological to the metaphysical stage might describe it as a (cognitive) movement from stress on gods to stress on entities.

We must ask questions with regard to Comte's work much like those we asked with regard to Frazer's. If we take the idea of a theological or metaphysical stage without any reservations, without a grain of salt, we may wonder how humans could possibly have survived with such approaches to the world. Was the theological stage *exclusively* theological? Were there no hints of other kinds of approaches to things; no small germs of science; no crude technologies? Was the metaphysical stage exclusively metaphysical? Like many other thinkers of some stature, Comte was actually often more perceptive than his system would suggest—if that system is understood very rigidly.

In Comte's view, the metaphysical stage is finally to be replaced by the positive or scientific. But this stage has not yet fully arrived, although it will arrive in the course of time. Comte saw modern society as being involved in "a great political and moral crisis" that was traceable to "intellectual anarchy" [1853, I:14–15]. This crisis or disorder was due to the *co-existence* of the theological, metaphysical, and positive philosophies. *One* of these would finally have to prevail and it would inevitably be the positive. The society of Comte's day, in his view, continued to suffer in the interim from cognitive hangovers from the past.

It is worth saying again that Comte was frequently more perceptive than a rigid interpretation of his system might suggest. If one follows his discussion of the so-called theological stage with care, for example, one notes that he is well aware that religion is more than a purely cognitive affair, involving as it does such things as ritual and ceremony. With all Comte's insistence that the positive philosophy alone must prevail, he himself created a Religion of Humanity [see particularly Comte 1877, IV] that supposedly had positive or scientific foundations. It is perhaps not too generous to recognize this effort to construct a religion as founded in a perception that not everything requisite for the existence of a society can come out of a cognitive system alone. Yet Comte's extreme cognitive emphasis strikes us again and again.

We are still constrained to ask whether the theological-to-metaphysical-to-positive movement is a correct lining up of modes of thought that follow out of one another in the sequence suggested. One could reasonably argue that this is an inadequate or even badly distorted sequence or only *one* among a number of historically significant sequences. Granted that there have been important cognitive influences of religion on science, *some* of the true antecedents of science are not to be found in "theology" or religion at all. (It may be granted as we discuss Comte, as when we discussed Frazer, that the *overall* history of mankind reveals some striking cognitive progress.)

As regards the extreme cognitive stress, Comte makes it quite plain in his account of the theological, metaphysical, and positive philosophies that in his view "intellectual development . . . governs every other" [1853, II:173]. Somehow, social life, or social organization generally, *emanates* from ideas. [On "emanationism," see Weber 1968a, pp. 141–145]. One hardly knows how else to put it. Comte is often most hazy about the character of the links between ideas and social organization, and it is difficult not to impute to him an "emanationist" view of their relationship. There is a strong temptation to see in this aspect of Comte's work a drive toward a "metaphysical" sociology! Ideas (theological, metaphysical, positive) in Comte's work operate rather too much as metaphysical entities that "establish" social states.

We must not overlook, however, sheer insistence on the correlation between ideas or idea-systems and social schemes. Polytheism "corresponds" to slavery. Fetishism is connected with the extermination of captives [1853,

II:228]. The positive philosophy and modern industrial society are very intimately connected. (This is one of Comte's more sensible endeavors in "connection.") In the long haul from theological to positive, we also are taken from a "military" to an "industrial" mode of organization [1853, II:178].

It is quite evident that Comte's social thought relies heavily on generous reflections on the historical process. History itself is a realm of necessity for him. Any important historical institution in particular, despite its possible shortcomings and despite an ultimate functional ineptitude, was in its time "unavoidable" (as well as "indispensable"). Any given social state is the necessary result of a preceding one and "the indispensable mover" of the one following [1853, II:83–84]. "Sociology has for each epoch in turn exhibited the present as the necessary outcome of the past" [1876, III:535]. History is characterized not only by inevitability but also by progress. Human society improves, and it must improve. Humanity often "needed" such and such in the past in order to guarantee something essential in the future. Hence, past events were in some mysterious way prospectively shaped so that they could perform their necessary functions for the future.

According to Comte, history is moving to a final state. In this state, a positive polity—a social constitution firmly grounded in science—will be in existence. It will be an outright utopia. Here, at the end of evolution, a benevolent capitalist group will show kindness toward the proletariat and a disposition to venerate a positivist or scientific priesthood. The workers, for their part, when adequately provided for, will be friendly toward capitalism. "When society is finally organized no other disturbance can arise" [1875, II:338]. Or, if utopia should not be quite unruffled, there will be ample resources for dealing with difficulties. Comte was optimistic. Progress, he averred, is the development of order. In the end, he appeared to be all for "order"; "development" seems to have gotten lost in the shuffle.

In the line of what is important for evolutionary theory, it is evident that we have here a not very successful attempt to achieve a major ordering of social stages by the heavy use of cognitive clues. This is not to deny that Comte made significant contributions in his time. He stimulated considerable interest in the history of science. Many of his comments about sociology remain provocative. His discussions of various historical phenomena, despite his biases and distortions, are often very shrewd. His analysis of the "critical" period of the modern Western civilization, extending over about five centuries, and his descriptions of Catholicism still lend a certain vitality to his pages. His inevitabilism and his insistence on the automatic quality of progress (with progress after all effectively stopped finally under a hypothetical utopia, which numerous critics have regarded as absurdly fanciful) are among the more serious shortcomings that nevertheless "date" his work.

Yet Comte's work patently typified certain elements in evolutionary thought. There were a number of lesser Comtes among nineteenth-century sociologists. Their errors and Comte's continue to be instructive.

For the sociologist interested in classical theories it might be well at this point to shift to our further consideration of Herbert Spencer. We seek, however, to review some important anthropological work and, in accordance with chronological sequence, we shall consider Lewis Henry Morgan before resuming the tale of Herbert Spencer.

Economic-Technological Interest and Holistic Evolution: Lewis Henry Morgan

An American lawyer and politician, Lewis Henry Morgan (1818–1881) also had the talent, the interest, and the energy to become one of his country's outstanding anthropologists.

In this essay Morgan concerns us for two reasons. One is that there is a strand in his work that allies him with those who have a strong economic-technological orientation in analyzing anything like evolution. Thus, Morgan writes, "It is . . . probable that the great epochs of human progress have been identified, more or less directly, with the enlargement of the sources of subsistence" [1964, originally 1877, p. 24]. Morgan distinguished five major sources of subsistence, each with large significance for the development of human society. He referred to subsistence on fruits and roots in a restricted area, subsistence on fish, subsistence through cereal and plant cultivation, subsistence on meat and milk, and "unlimited subsistence through field agriculture" [1964, pp. 24–30].

The subtitle of his famous book, *Ancient Society*, in which these modes of subsistence are distinguished was, as noted earlier, *Researches in the Lines of Human Progress from Savagery through Barbarism to Civilization*. The book divided savagery into lower, middle, and upper stages and made the same tripartite division for barbarism. The connections of subsistence and these stages are suggested when, for example, Morgan tells us that cereal and plant cultivation occurs as we leave savagery and enter the lower phase of barbarism.

Morgan was enormously impressed with the importance of iron for human development. "Furnished with iron tools, capable of holding both an edge and a point, mankind were certain of attaining to civilization. The production of iron was the event of events in human experience, without a parallel . . ." [1964, p. 43]. And again: "The process of smelting iron ore was the invention of inventions . . . beside which all other inventions and discoveries held a subordinate position" [1964, p. 457]. Iron was in fact entirely indispensable for the emergence of the stage of civilization.

The first point, then, is quite plain: Morgan is one of the looming figures in anthropology who encouraged the economic-technological stress in discussing evolutionary shifts. This no doubt was a main reason for his well-known influence on Karl Marx and Frederick Engels. Engels wrote a small volume entitled *The Origin of the Family, Private Property, and the State*, in which he drew heavily on Morgan, although adding some points of his own. Engels actually stated that "Morgan in his own way had discovered afresh in America the materialistic conception of history discovered by Marx . . . and in his comparison of barbarism and civilization it had led him, in the main points, to the same conclusions as Marx." Engels noted further that "Morgan is the first man who with expert knowledge has attempted to introduce a definite order into the history of primitive man . . ." [Engels 1942, pp. 5, 19].

The second point on which Morgan is of interest for us has to do with an observation made repeatedly and insistently by critics of nineteenth-century social-evolutionary theorists. It is that those theorists argued that "all societies go through the same stages." Consideration of Morgan gives us the opportunity to clarify an essential distinction here. The following crucial and pertinent pair of sentences are from Morgan.

Since mankind were one in origin, their career has been essentially one, running in different but uniform channels upon all continents, and very similarly in all the tribes and nations of mankind down to the same status of advancement. It follows that the history and experience of the American Indian tribes represent, more or less nearly, the history and experience of our own remote ancestors when in corresponding conditions [1964, pp. 6–7].

This may sound most suspicious. All societies would indeed seem to "go through the same stages" but this has been challenged again and again as a gratuitous assumption. If one takes some feature, such as a form of marriage, from Society A—let us call the feature X—and then talks about Society B, which has, say, a more "advanced" form of the same feature—designated Y—it does not follow that Society B ever had the particular feature in the particular form (X) that it shows in Society A. X did not necessarily precede Y in Society B. There is no evidence that Society A will ever proceed to form Y. There has sometimes been a careless taking of "pieces" or social patterns or structures out of their particular historical series and making unfounded assumptions about identical *sequences* of such "pieces" or patterns or structures across societies.

This careless procedure has been described as "the comparative method," with the implication, of course, that it involves a quite invalid way of "comparing." Goldenweiser contended a half century ago that this comparative method assumed precisely the identity of developmental stages in different tribes or societies, and commented further:

> But is not the assumption of the identity of developmental stages in different tribes one of the fundamental principles of social evolution? Thus the theory of evolution must be accepted as a postulate before the comparative method can be used. It follows that the results of this method cannot be regarded as proof but merely as a series of illustrations of a postulated evolutionary theory [1922, pp. 22–23; cf. Nisbet 1969, *passim*; Mandelbaum 1971, pp. 265–266].

Goldenweiser has a point, but just how does the point apply? Much nineteenth-century evolutionary thought was of a very broad, *holistic* character. The evolutionists were interested in laying down certain grand lines of development. Thus, in reference to the passage from Morgan, beginning "Since mankind were one in origin . . ." (quoted above), Service suggests that Morgan "meant nothing more than that wherever barbarism (defined by the traits of horticulture or pastoralism) was found, a general stage of hunting-gathering society (savagery) had preceded it and that stages of both had preceded civilization on continents that had achieved civilization. Such a judgment is attested by archeology now as well as by common sense . . ." [Service 1968, V:223].

The criticism Goldenweiser makes would have application in cases of specific kinds of studies concentrated on particular societies throughout their course, or on particular social structures or institutions within particular societies. The evolutionists might have defended themselves against Goldenweiser, certainly, at least as far as their holistic, grand-style work was concerned. Morris Ginsberg, writing an Introduction for the 1965 reprint of his book of 1915 with Hobhouse and Wheeler on *The Material Culture and Social Institutions of the Simpler Peoples*, protests, "Why anyone ever thought that a theory of social evolution must necessarily assume that all peoples developed in a uniform manner it is now difficult to say" [Hobhouse, Wheeler, & Ginsberg 1965, p. vii]. If Ginsberg meant that support for holistic evolutionary views does not necessarily imply support for rigidly uniform schemes of development for various particular institutions or social patterns or structures, he was certainly justified.

In this whole matter of societies going through the same stages, this is a good juncture at which to note that Herbert Spencer is not the very easy target he appeared to be to some critics of his work. Spencer saw that the course of development in detail is by no means everywhere the same. He recognized clearly that specializations and differentiations in medicine, in surgery, and in pharmacy, for example, are not similar everywhere. He remarked, directly to the point, that ". . . like other kinds of progress, social progress is not linear but divergent and re-divergent . . . multiplying groups have tended ever to acquire differences, now major and now minor: there have arisen genera and species of societies" [1899, III:196–197, 331].

As Service effectively reminds us [1968, p. 223], what may now seem like holistic truisms on the part of such nineteenth-century anthropologists as Morgan were worth stating. In Morgan's day, "theories of degeneration and catastrophe were still opposed to evolutionism," and there was point in setting forth some rather simple evolutionary views.

Types of Societies—
An Evolutionary Dialectic:
Herbert Spencer

Herbert Spencer (1820–1903) was a major figure in nineteenth-century thought. His range over the sciences was impressive; his preoccupation with evolution was intense and persistent. There is currently something of a renewal of attention to Spencer's considerable contribution to sociological analysis. We follow Spencer's interest in discriminating types of societies and then develop the dialectical bent that is present in his thought, although he never gave it that name.

Types of Societies

"Social evolution," Spencer observed, "begins with small simple aggregates." But "it progresses by the clustering of these into larger aggregates," and then, "after being consolidated, such clusters are united with others like themselves into still larger aggregates" [1899, II:550]. A simple society is one that forms ". . . a single working whole unsubjugated to any other, and of which the parts co-operate, with or without a regulating centre, for certain public ends" [1899, I:551]. A compound society is one which to greater or lesser degree has passed into a state in which the simple groups "have their respective chiefs under a supreme chief." Doubly compound societies are formed by the recompounding of compound groups; that is to say, they are "societies in which many governments [of the compound type] have become subject to a still higher government" [1899, I:553]. Still higher compounding follows the same logic to yield trebly compound societies.

Crucial elements in this classification have to do with whether headship is stable or unstable (or occasional) and with whether the societies listed are settled, semisettled, or nomadic. The great civilized nations all fall under the head of the trebly compound. "Ancient Mexico, the Assyrian Empire, the Egyptian Empire, the Roman Empire, Great Britain, France, Germany, Italy, Russia, may severally be regarded as having reached" the trebly compound stage—"or perhaps," Spencer added, "in some cases, a still higher stage" [1899, I:554]. A criterion of increasing complexity is obviously being used.

Spencer's work here is suggestive and sensible enough to merit the few words we have allowed it, and clearly what he did is susceptible of elaboration. More of modern interest attaches, however, to his famous distinction between militant and industrial societies. Here, too, Spencer's interest was in a large evolutionary shift.

Militant societies are antagonistic to other societies. They are strongly characterized by the coercion of their human units into various combined actions. In those societies, ". . . as the soldier's will is so suspended that he becomes in everything the agent of his officer's will; so is the will of the citizen in all transactions, private and public, overruled by that of the government." Further, the social structure adapted to dealing with environing inimical societies is ". . . under a centralized regulating system, to which all the parts are completely subject; just as in the individual organism the outer organs are completely subject to the chief nervous centre" [1899, I:564]. It may be noted by the way that the consolidation of simple into compound aggregates "habitually" (Spencer's own rather vague word) is a consequence of war, which, when maintained over time, "evolves a centralized authority with its coercive institutions" [1899, I:565].

In industrial societies, there is free combining or associating of individuals, who are governed representatively. "In place of the doctrine that the duty of obedience to the governing agent is unqualified, there arises the doctrine that the will of the citizens is supreme and the governing agent exists merely to carry out their will" [1899, I:568]. Further, in industrial societies all trading transactions are effected on a basis of free exchange. Relationships typically arise in which there is mutual rendering of services and the parties involved in transactions are not subordinated to one another [1899, I:569].

Coercion is opposed to free employment. Compulsion is opposed to contract. Status too, is opposed to contract, as action based on one's standing or position in a group is opposed to action based on explicit agreements with little regard to position. The more pronounced a society's militancy, the greater the scorn felt for occupations other than that of the soldier [1899, III: 367].

Much else is associated with the militant-industrial contrast. Thus, militant societies tend toward polygamy; industrial ones, toward monogamy. Under militant systems, the gods tend to be ferocious; under industrial ones, loving and kind.

Although Spencer undoubtedly conceived that there was a broad evolutionary shift from militant to industrial types of societies, this is not invariably a simple, straightforward movement, and he had anxieties about the renascence of militant tendencies that he discerned late in the nineteenth century. Armaments and national bellicosity, among other things, disturbed him. Writing of his own day, he referred to "our present transitional state, semi-militant and semi-industrial" [1899, III:551]. The militant type can indeed turn toward the industrial, but the industrial can also "retrograde" toward the militant. There clearly can also be mixtures of militant and industrial elements in concrete societies.

The contrast of militant and industrial is complicated by what one must call Spencer's ideological opposition to state control. He felt that in his day "the individual withers and the State is more and more." He saw "multiplied meddling" by the state in his day, as well as "coercive legislation" involving, for example, governmental invasion of the private citizen's purse in order to obtain support for public education. He feared the prospective establishment of a "state in which no man can do what he likes but every man must do what he is told" [1899, III:603–605]. Accordingly, militancy loomed ominously both in a sense of a threat of spreading internal coercion within modern nations and in a sense of what Spencer would have regarded as unfortunate military undertakings abroad. But the militant-industrial contrast might perhaps have been developed more richly and powerfully had Spencer engaged in careful critical evaluation of his own unrelentingly adverse stance toward "statism" and "officialdom."

It is worth noting that Spencer was quite outspoken about what he considered pernicious militancy undertakings. He was convinced England still had an archaic militant hangover that was manifested in constantly "carrying on small wars with uncivilized tribes" [1898, II:632]. He could write, "We need teaching that it is impossible to join injustice and brutality abroad with justice and humanity at home" [1898, II:642]. It may be added that Spencer's evolutionary optimism was not destroyed by what he took to be the advancing militancy of his time, but the latter surely helped make him cautious. As he approached the end of the last volume of his *Principles of Sociology* he urged, as we noted earlier, that "there is no uniform ascent from lower to higher" [1899, III:609].

An Evolutionary Dialectic

Although, in Spencer's view, only harm could come from war today [1898, II:664–665], he still thought war had been useful or "functional" in the earlier course of social evolution. Here we note a dialectical or paradoxical twist in his thought that is well worth our attention. Both in his *Principles of Sociology* and in his remarkable shorter book, *The Study of Sociology*, Spencer contended that war has been historically responsible for consolidations that create large societies. Once large societies are actually in existence, industrial progress is furthered. Hostilities are then broken by intervals of peace. The division of labor can more effectively be carried out. Historically, or in evolutionary context, war (and this is an eminently "dialetical" sort of contention) contains the seeds of its own destruction, since in the slow course of development it ". . . brings about a social aggregation which furthers that industrial state at variance with war." Spencer added that "nothing but war could bring about the social aggregation" [1924, originally 1873, p. 176].

We do not need to speculate about the Olympian detachment (if that is an appropriate phrase here) that can make palatable to the great sociologist much misery and suffering on the ground that it did finally work to the benefit of mankind. Nor do we want to raise close empirical questions about Spencer's correlation of war and the consolidation of societies whose further development then tends to eliminate war, although we would incline to concede a rough justification to his relevant views.

It is the precise character of his historical or evolutionary dialectic that now interests us. In Spencer's outlook, many of the social establishments or institutions that humans have reared and which are exceedingly useful or "functional" were originally given at least some support on the motivational side by greed, lust, spite, and the like. They still performed their beneficent functions nevertheless. In a manner of speaking they constitute a house that humans have constructed with less than worthy aims in view, but which in principle can *now* be sustained and further built up with newer and worthier aims. Spencer was acutely aware that various activities might be *set* in motion by aims of one sort and then *kept* going by aims of another sort. Quite like a modern organizational theorist, Spencer observed that ". . . by the histories of organizations of whatever kind, we are shown that the purpose originally subserved by some arrangement is not always the purpose eventually subserved" [1898, II:429].

The point was touched on again by Spencer in his presentation of a kind of evolutionary function of asceticism. He believed that asceticism developed out of the wish to propitiate evil spiritual beings. Even as asceticism is found among ourselves, Spencer further believed, there may be glimpsed in it the latent notion that a supernatural being is pleased by mortifications voluntarily endured and displeased by the spectacle of gratifications. These would surely not be thought of as especially gracious or ethically lovely roots. "Considered in the abstract, asceticism is indefensible," Spencer writes accordingly. But, he also observed, if we regard the self-infliction of suffering, bodily or mental, not in the light of "absolute" ethics but rather in the light of "relative ethics"—as a human "educational regimen"—then "we shall see that it has had a use, and perhaps a great use" [1899, III:143].

Asceticism has helped "in developing the ability to postpone present to future," for Spencer saw it as the common feature of ascetic acts that they involve submission to pain with a view to avoiding future greater pain or giving up a present pleasure in order to obtain a larger future one. Thus asceticism has functioned historically to train mankind to defer gratification and to aid to attain greater gratification by deferment.

Once again it would appear that ethically ugly or dubious motives have been at the historical foundations of certain structures or of prescribed modes of action. Once the structures or modes of action are in being, however, they have a value independent of the motives that helped to rear them.

In part, what is involved in all this bears comparison with the famous concluding paragraph of Charles Darwin's *The Origin of Species,* in which a critical sentence runs: "Thus, from the war of nature, from famine and death, the most exalted object which we are capable of conceiving, namely, the production of the higher animals, directly follows" [1936, originally 1859, p. 374]. Spencer and Darwin are in a way at one. The higher animals, one might say, come out of a primeval muck and slime, out of what seem unpromising materials, out of a severe struggle for existence. So, too, "higher" structures and moral prescriptions come out of a "muck and slime" of "low" or dubious motives. Spencer also may here be said to be adding the point that new wine can be poured into old bottles; or, that an old "house" can be maintained and even further built up for reasons different from those that had to do with its original construction.

Such views as these were not unique to Spencer as a social theorist. It should be noted briefly that intimations of them are to be found in the work of Spencer's contemporary, Henry Sumner Maine [1822–1888]. Maine was trained in law and was for some time a professor of law at Cambridge. He asserted that ". . . the warning can never be too often repeated that the grand source of mistake in questions of jurisprudence is the impression that those reasons which actuate us at the present moment, in the maintenance of an existing institution, have necessarily anything in common with the sentiment in which the institution originated." In discussing the Roman invention of the will, Maine remarked that ". . . we must be careful not to attribute to it in its earliest shape the functions which have attended it in more recent times" [1959, originally 1861, pp. 157, 161]. The affinity of this with what we have been discussing in Spencer needs no elaboration.

We are not yet at the end of Spencer's historical or evolutionary dialectic or paradoxical stance. His *The*

Study of Sociology contains a striking exposition of the point that a developed structure can stand in the way of, or impede further, improved or more adaptive structures. An adaptation that has been made already may involve an "investment" on which one may not want to lose, and hence one adaptation may stand in the way of another and more effective one. To illustrate this point in the social sphere, Spencer dwelt on appliances for locomotion. His stress is that existing arrangements may impede better ones. Passing to railways in particular, he wrote:

Observe how the inconveniently-narrow gauge . . . has become an insuperable obstacle to any better gauge. Observe, also, how the type of carriage, which was derived from the body of a stage-coach . . . having become established, it is immensely difficult now to introduce the more convenient type later established in America; where they profited by our experience but were not hampered by our adopted plans. The enormous capital invested in our stock of carriages cannot be sacrificed. Gradually to introduce carriages of the American type, by running them along with those of our type, would be very difficult, because of our many partings and joinings of trains. And thus we are obliged to go on with a type that is inferior [1924, pp. 59–60].

Spencer here pointed to "the penalty of taking the lead" and the frequent advantage of the latecomer, who, being late, has no investment in obsolete forms but may be able to start anew with the best available. Thorstein Veblen's *Imperial Germany and the Industrial Revolution*, with little doubt, drew on Spencer's insight. Veblen indicated how Germany, in going in heavily for industrialization after 1870, learned its basic industrial ways from England, which had begun to industrialize earlier, while Germany had the great advantage of not needing always to invest in old industrial forms with which England was effectively "stuck." The penalty of taking the lead can also be phrased as the advantage of the newcomer. Veblen's thesis in *Imperial Germany* involves more than this idea but it depends heavily upon it. Veblen even adduced the very example of the narrow gauge of the railways of England or Great Britain, which we have just seen Spencer adducing [Veblen 1939, p. 130].

This is one of the points at which Spencer's historical or evolutionary dialectic or paradoxical argument clearly becomes relevant to certain problems of modernization. The whole matter, indeed, is important enough for us to note, more than casually, ways in which it has come up since Spencer's time.

The revolutionary Leon Trotsky stressed a law of combined development, by which he meant to suggest a backward country's tendency to combine the old with the new in its development. As such a country begins to develop more toward modern industrial forms, it can borrow from industrially more advanced countries. But it need not reproduce the step-by-step development that occurred in those countries. It may skip whole series of intermediate stages. Thus: "Savages throw away their bows and arrows for rifles all at once, without traveling the road which lay between those two weapons in the past." Moreover, Trotsky remarks in particular that ". . . the fact that Germany and the United States have now economically outstripped England was made possible by the very backwardness of their development. England played too long [for its own good] the role of capitalist pathfinder." Just before World War I, Trotsky contended, one could see in Russia's relatively very considerable engagement of its industrial workers in huge enterprises an instance of a greatly advanced industrial feature in a backward country whose agricultural circumstances were still reminiscent of the seventeenth century. The old was indeed combined with the new. According to Trotsky, Russia employed twice as many of its industrial workers in huge enterprises as the United States did of its industrial workers [1932, I:4–5, 6, 9, 10, 14, 50–51].

The relevant points made by Spencer, Veblen, and Trotsky need not be interpreted as eternal truths. The latecomer does not always have an advantage. The basic idea of the penalty of taking the lead is nevertheless extremely suggestive for theories of change, and this suggestiveness has been recognized in analysis of economic development [see Gerschenkron 1962, 1968], and in wider-ranging historical work.

Such wider-ranging historical work is exemplified particularly in the fourth volume of Arnold Toynbee's *Study of History*. Starting with reference to pertinent biological phenomena, as Spencer had done, Toynbee sought to show how (in Gerald Heard's words) the very "success of efficiency" can lead to "extinction." (Heard wrote, "A creature which has become perfectly adapted to its environment, an animal whose whole capacity and vital force is concentrated and expended in succeeding here and now, has nothing left over with which to respond to any radical change.") Toynbee drew extensively on the history of military techniques to reinforce this point. But on his way he also reviewed the case of England in relation to latecomers in industrial competition (such as Germany, the United States, and Japan) in terms that fit Veblen's treatment in *Imperial Germany*. England "rested on its oars," to use one of Toynbee's apt expressions. It is well to make this reference to economic contexts again, but

Toynbee carried his relevant arguments well beyond the economic sphere. In his words, a people can "idolize" or make a fetish of "an ephemeral technique," which will actually prove inadequate as others, free of frozen commitments, adopt better techniques. But the techniques idolized need not be confined to devices strictly pertinent to the economic sphere. [Toynbee 1939, IV:423–465. The quotation, above, from Heard, is given by Toynbee IV:424, from Heard 1935, pp. 66–67.]

The story could be carried on. We shall merely note Walter Bagehot's comment that ". . . the very institutions which most aid at step number one are precisely those which most impede at step number two" [1948, pp. 153–154. Cf. Toynbee 1939, IV:134, footnote]. We shall also simply allude to Max Weber's recognition of the advantages that *may* paradoxically appertain to backwardness [1968, II:688; III:987].

Reason and Evolution

A word about reason and human volition will round out our account of Spencer. There is in Spencer's writings more than a hint that reason is somehow implicit in the evolutionary process. Much that was beneficial or functional in human establishments arose unintentionally or without anticipation, by Spencer's analysis. He could indeed write brilliantly about unintended or unanticipated consequences. But, in intimate connection with this, he often gives the impression of an observer who sees the process of evolution at work in human societies (as elsewhere) and relies on *this* to bring about results that humans might regard as thoroughly desirable.

Spencer's great American counterpart, William Graham Sumner (1840–1910), once wrote a piece entitled "The Absurd Effort to Make the World Over." He argued in this that we are all products of our time and cannot get out of it; that "the tide [of human history] will not be changed by us" but rather will "swallow" both us and our experiments; and that it is entire folly to make blueprints for a new social world [1934, I:104–106]. This reflects, in good part, Spencerian views [see, however, Stark 1961:521]. The Evolutionary Process compasses all. Reason and human volition might even intervene dangerously and harmfully where that process is at work. The next thinker taken up, namely Hobhouse, certainly differs from Spencer in regard to this matter.

Morals, Evolution, and Reason: Leonard T. Hobhouse

Leonard T. Hobhouse (1864–1929), like Comte and Spencer, was both a philosopher and a sociologist. He was the first Martin White Professor of sociology at the University of London and was a prolific writer on ethical, political, and sociological subjects.

One of the last great works that may be said to be in the nineteenth-century evolutionary tradition in social science was Hobhouse's *Morals in Evolution* [1929]. Given our limited concerns with Hobhouse, we overlook numerous valuable points in this work. Some of Hobhouse's accounts of ethical and religious developments, as in his concise study of Buddhism [1929, pp. 477–485], and some of his sociological analyses [e.g., 1929, pp. 617–618], which adumbrate later functionalist ideas, would be worth comment if we were reviewing his contribution as a whole. But we are interested only in his broad thesis and in his broadly stated view of the prospects of human reason in affecting the evolutionary process.

Morals in Evolution originally appeared in 1905, but it went through a number of editions. From 1915 on Hobhouse could draw, for it, from the other work he published in that year together with Wheeler and Ginsberg, entitled *The Material Culture and Social Institutions of the Simpler Peoples*. The latter book afforded him useful information in *Morals in Evolution* and helped him organize its materials.

In *Morals in Evolution* Hobhouse undertakes a very ambitious survey of morality and ethics at different social levels. He operates holistically, by way of comparison of different peoples who are loosely fitted onto a line of ethical development. He was clearly inclined to hope that his "comparative study," provided it was "firmly based on recorded facts," would have validity even "if the theory of evolution were shattered" [1929, Preface, p. v]. He observed that to deal with ethical evolution "in fullness," it would be desirable to have "a continuous ethical history of mankind throughout the ages" [1929, p. 25]. This was not available, and Hobhouse had his uncertainties about the holistic procedure in the field of ethical development.

The interest expressed in Hobhouse's book is in both explicitly ethical or philosophically expressed views regarding morality, and in morality as embodied in custom. Not only primitive peoples, but the people of ancient Egypt, Israel, Greece, and Rome, and the modern world figure in Hobhouse's voluminous pages. In the first part of his book he covered law and justice, the position of women, class relations, actions bearing on property, and poverty. In the second part Hobhouse dealt with ethical and religious philosophies.

Perhaps above all one gets the impression from Hobhouse's book of a dual struggle—a struggle to believe that mankind has actually shown a general advance in the line of higher ethics or morality; and a struggle to believe that man has a genuine chance to control his own destiny. Hobhouse was vastly informed, and naive, easy belief hardly characterizes him. Like Spencer, he was acutely aware of unanticipated consequences. Thus he wrote that even "reforms most deliberately planned and most carefully thought out have a hundred unexpected reactions over and above the direct effect which they were designed to produce" [1919, pp. 20–21]. He was well apprised that this did not always work out to human advantage.

Further, Hobhouse plainly had some fear that humanitarianism might be, as he put it, a temporary product of the eighteenth and nineteenth centuries. One might be skeptical of the progress of humanitarianism after 1870 [1929, pp. 611–612]. Hobhouse suggested that Victorian humanitarian progress in his time might be ". . . relaxing its efforts and giving place to the creed of force and the self-centered will" [1929, p. 631]. This, too, is of course quite reminiscent of the Spencer disturbed by the recrudescence of bellicose behavior on the international scene.

Still it is evident that Hobhouse *wanted* to believe in the reality of ethical or moral progress. Even with his qualms, it is fair to say that he did believe in it to some extent. He observed at the end of *Morals in Evolution* that the further development of society—assuming that he had read rightly and could project correctly from the general evolutionary record—was "destined to fall within the scope of an organizing intelligence" and thus "to be removed from the play of blind force to the sphere of rational order." Again he had his reservations and hesitations, but still allowed his optimism some scope as he wrote that the ". . . slowly wrought out dominance of mind in things is the central fact of evolution" [1929, p. 637]. From the general tone of his argument, one might well infer that he was ambivalent about this statement and could have confessed that the spectacle of the human evolutionary process might be so construed as to raise a *hope* about the "dominance" of mind or reason, but not a thoroughly firm conviction.

But it is evident in any case that for Hobhouse there is nothing like unqualified reliance on the Evolutionary Process to bring about things in human society that reason and good will might project. On the contrary, the evolutionary goal to look forward to is the "self-conscious evolution of humanity."

Hobhouse was hardly the only sociologist that was much influenced by evolutionary thought who looked hopefully to "mind" or human rationality for guidance in further human development. The well-known American sociologist Lester Frank Ward (1841–1913), attributed great significance to "telesis," or purpose in guiding the social process. He referred to "the conscious method" [1903, p. 463] of controlling social energy and entertained high hopes for the enlightenment that was to come from mass education.

With Hobhouse, we get a sense of being at the end of a line. It is true that a number of the older evolutionary concerns persist in the work of the next theorist to be considered, Émile Durkheim, especially in his work on the division of labor. Nevertheless, with Durkheim we enter, generally speaking, into the stream of distinctively "modern" social theory. Durkheim is almost invariably put beside Max Weber (and often also with Karl Marx and Vilfredo Pareto) as one of the grand initiators of the sociological enterprise more or less as we understand it now. He is accordingly treated separately from the previous theorists.

Dualistic
Development Theory:
Emile Durkheim

Émile Durkheim (1858–1917) was appointed professor of sociology and education at the Sorbonne in 1902. In addition to the early work scrutinized here, he was the author of widely acclaimed studies of suicide and of primitive religion.

In *The Division of Labor in Society,* Durkheim discusses a general movement in societies from mechanical to organic solidarity. He argues that in primitive societies mechanical solidarity prevails. In these societies, the individual is bound directly to society itself, in the limiting case without any intermediary. The "conscience collective"—consisting of the beliefs and sentiments common to the members of a group—has great force. Where organic solidarity prevails, the individual is dependent on society in virtue of his dependence on the "parts" of which it consists. The conscience collective does not have the same significance that it does in primitive groups.

Under mechanical solidarity, there is little division of labor. Men are only slightly differentiated by belonging to *different* social groups ("parts") within a larger social set-up. "Solidarity which comes from likenesses is at its maximum when the collective conscience completely envelops our whole conscience and coincides in all points with it" [Durkheim 1933, p. 130]. Personality or individuality "vanishes" here. As Durkheim remarks, we are not "ourselves" but rather we are "the collective life." Under organic solidarity, the conscience collective comes much less near to taking up the entirety of the individual or of his mental and emotional life. Complete originality is certainly not possible under organic solidarity either. As social specialization occurs and men and women are taken up in clearly differentiated occupations, they do conform to usages, "to practices which are common to [their] whole professional brotherhood." However, the situation here is still quite different from the one that prevails where the conscience collective is extremely powerful, "where society completely controls us" [1933, p. 131].

Given the likeness of its several human units, a society in which mechanical solidarity prevails has a segmental character and its components rather readily separate and can sustain independent existence, just as among lower organisms it may be the case that "cut up" or deliberately separated parts may sustain independent life. (One must think again of Spencer.) Modern societies, however, have a complex division of labor. Given, precisely, such phenomena as different groups involved in different occupations, human beings are differently stamped. The "parts" of society become highly interdependent and cannot sustain separate life. Highly specialized occupations must service one another. Cities can hardly be cut off from a countryside that supplies them with food. Solidarity is now organic rather than mechanical. Men and groups within the same general society still tend to be held together by shared beliefs and values. Yet, it is well to repeat, those shared beliefs and values no longer come so near (on the subjective side) to exhausting the entire mental content, the whole consciousness of human beings. Too much complication and specialization of thought and sentiment have occurred because of membership in specialized groups for this to happen.

Durkheim knew that there are distinctive social vulnerabilities that come with organic solidarity. Overarching, "umbrella"-like values, rules, rights, duties that are supposed to function to "hold society together" where it gets very complex and specialized (in the manner of so-called modern societies) may not function effectively for various reasons. The overarching elements may become too "thin" and precarious. Derangements and terrible conflicts may occur.

But if the division of labor does produce solidarity, this is so, for Durkheim, just because it creates among men and women a whole scheme of rights and duties, "an entire system of rights and duties which link them together in a durable way," in Durkheim's own words. The division of labor gives rise to "rules which assure pacific and regular concourse of divided functions" [1933, p. 406]. It is *always* a matter of stress, too, that the division of labor develops individuality. It makes the individual an autonomous source of action, or at least a being who is released from the stereotyping of a "simple" society.

The Division of Labor, despite its merits, is a much

flawed book. Durkheim associated repressive or criminal law with primitive society and mechanical solidarity, and what he called restitutive law with modern society and organic solidarity. The evidence indicates that this was far too great a simplification [see especially Nisbet 1974, chapter 4]. Again one may point to Durkheim's consideration of "abnormal" forms of the division of labor as disappointingly brief and argue as Lukes has done [1972, p. 174], contending that this very characterization as abnormal tended to inhibit an adequate inquiry into their causes—"especially given the evolutionary optimism Durkheim espoused at this stage."

It has just been noted that Durkheim greatly oversimplified in the matter of law and its relation to societies. The central difficulties of Durkheim's dualistic evolutionary analysis, indeed, stem from oversimplification on each side of the mechanical-organic contrast. Preindustrial societies, generally, are characterized by a great deal of interdependence and reciprocity, in the way of kinship and ritual and political alliance—far more so than Durkheim seems to have realized [Lukes 1972, p. 159]. On the other hand, in societies that have industrialized, there are elements of solidarity and group integration that are still of considerable importance. As Merton suggests with respect to such "modern" societies, it is still true that there are unities or solidarities that are substantially achieved "through appeals to common sentiments" [1934, 319–328]. Primordial, ancient ties of "blood, faith, land and consciousness of kind" have by no means altogether lapsed in modern societies. The point has been well argued for example by Greeley [1971, e.g. p. 183], who adduces some, although far from all, of the persuasive evidence that can be assembled for it.

Even in its considerable oversimplification, Durkheim's dualistic-evolutionary thesis remains an important one. When necessary qualifications have been made, the residue is valuable. Toennies had a point, after all, when he made his statement (roughly paralleling Durkheim's main thesis in *The Division of Labor*) to the effect that ". . . in the course of history, folk culture has given rise to the civilization of the state" [1940, p. 263]. But the significance of Durkheim's work goes beyond such general statements in accordance with his own dualistic-evolutionary stress.

Durkheim's work evidently influenced Parsons' effort to develop a so-called paradigm of evolutionary change [Parsons 1966, pp. 21–23]. Parsons is concerned, among other things, with how it may come about that groups of different backgrounds and different cultures may come to live together under the terms of a normative scheme that is necessarily relatively *general*. It must be relatively general since it must appeal to groups that differ in their specific cultural character, but that yet may also show some generic, overall cultural features more or less of the nature of common denominators that can serve to bind them together. One kind of social unity could exist when all members of society (for practical purposes) were Catholics. Another kind of unity came into being (even if very painfully and slowly) when the same society had to contain, say, Catholics *and* Jews *and* Protestants.

There is no occasion here to inquire into various important empirical issues as to just what "holds" large societies (or any societies) "together." It is enough to note merely that sociologists continue to take very seriously questions bearing on the role of normative features, of moral standards of the most overarching kind (technically, "values"), of standards of less overarching kind, of beliefs, in such "holding together." Because of Durkheim's consideration of such questions in his much too sweeping yet incisive *Division of Labor*, it remains a significant book. Durkheim was obviously greatly concerned about "integration"—precisely, about the "holding together" of societies with highly differentiated components or "parts." However critical Durkheim was of Spencer, the latter's work was indispensable for his own. *The Division of Labor* unmistakably recalls Spencer's world of differentiations and integrations. A concern with "integration," incidentally, is an analytical or theoretical concern that does *not* necessarily commit a theorist to the view that a society simply must be held together somehow, "no matter what," nor to the absurd notion that there can be no "disintegrating" features at work in a social system.

Cyclical Theories of Change: Vilfredo Pareto and Pitirim A. Sorokin

It has already been suggested that evolutionary and cyclical theories are not necessarily incompatible in all respects. Moreover, particular theorists who set out cyclical views may also harbor evolutionary ones. (Some cyclical theory has been motivated, however, by antagonism to the evolutionary outlook.) Furthermore, a theorist may be more restrained about his cyclical bias than our designation of him as a "cyclical theorist" might suggest. Sorokin, for example, saw nothing "necessary," in the cyclical course of culture that we shall find him expounding. Yet, given such reservations, there is a strong cyclical accent in certain important social theorists, as we shall see in the cases of Pareto and of Sorokin himself.

Pareto on the Circulation of Elites

An Italian nobleman, Vilfredo Pareto (1848–1923) was one of the foremost economists of his day and was for some years a professor at the University of Lausanne. Pareto's major sociological work, *The Mind and Society* [1916], appeared late in his career but evidently was written while he was still in full possession of his intellectual powers.

The cyclical notions presented by Pareto cannot be discussed without a fair amount of reference to his technical views and basic terms. It is important to note that he regarded society in "social system" terms. He saw society as a system of interdependent elements in which there is a constant tendency to equilibrium, restoring the system to its "normal" state when "extraordinary" modifications occur. He wrote that if some modification of the system is induced artificially, "at once a reaction will take place, tending to restore the changing form to its original state as modified by normal change" [1935, originally 1916, IV:1435]. The words—"as modified by normal change"—are particularly worth noting. Pareto also knew, of course, that there can be very large modification in social systems, on the line of major structural changes [see Parsons 1968, XI:413].

Within the social system, Pareto gave much attention to what he called residues and derivations. The residues are manifestations of basic human sentiments. Pareto observed these manifestations by examining large numbers of propositions, statements made by human beings in all sorts of contexts (political, economic, military, sexual, and so on). The real interest is ultimately in the *sentiments* that the residues manifest, and in casual usage residues refer to the sentiments themselves. The reader may discern where residue is used in the sense of manifestation of sentiment, or in the sense of sentiment itself.

In dealing with residues or sentiments, Pareto operated by a certain procedure or method. In a way, the procedure or method is extremely simple, and it is also extremely audacious. Pareto essentially drew on his great historical knowledge to yield him large numbers of statements that have been made by human beings throughout history and which he probed for their content, to see what sentiments they manifested. When related sets of statements were thus examined by him, Pareto arrived at decisions about the underlying or constant elements in or "behind" those statements. What is the underlying, the "genuine" manifestation of a sentiment (or what is the sentiment itself) that we discern when all the "verbiage" is swept away? What is left over—what is the *residue*—when secondary, variable elements are removed? The variable elements are labeled "derivations" by Pareto. "Residues abide," he observed, "while derivations change" [1935, II:829].

The warning must be given that, at best, in a short treatment one can render only a bare notion of Pareto's complex view of the residues. For a very rough understanding of the sense of the residues, one might think of a Mr. X who complains ceaselessly about his wife. On Monday it seems Mrs. X does not keep the house clean. On Tuesday she does not keep herself clean. On Wednesday it appears she neglects the children. On Thursday she is extravagant. On Friday she is insulting to Mr. X's friends. On Saturday she spurns his sexual advances. On Sunday she is sullen all day. It might be legitimate to conclude that there is a constant here, something residual or left over after various "words" are stripped away: Mr. X *just does not like his wife.* The complaints might be said to "derive from this dislike, and if one complaint does not sound plausible, even to Mr. X, another is sure to be forthcoming.

But this, we suggest, affords no more than a crude intimation of Pareto's relevant thought. He begins with propositions and "theories" (to which Mr. X's complaints are somewhat analogous) and he is interested in humans-in-history or humans-in-society. He may go, for his data, to parliaments and religious circles and the writings of philosophers and sociologists. He wants to know what "moves" humans in many social situations. We cannot always be sure how right or wrong his conclusions may be. His shrewdness and knowledge are great, and without doubt he often performs significant analyses in his treatment of residues and derivations. But there was no thoroughly systematic procedure available for what he undertook. It is possible that, in some important cases, others might come to different conclusions from Pareto's. They might discern somewhat different residues. They might see derivations where he saw residues and vice-versa.

As we have said, residues point to sentiments or are manifestations of sentiments (or may be in loose usage understood to be sentiments). If one follows Pareto at all closely, however, one soon sees that "sentiment" is a very large "box" indeed. The residues sometimes involve values or normative elements; yet they show highly variable components whose character may appear elusive, and they may involve instinct in the biological sense, as in the case of the sex residue [but see Lopreato 1965, pp. 7–9; 1975]. We can only mention this complicating circumstance.

In the huge agglomeration of human statements that Pareto actually reviewed and analyzed, he discriminated six classes of residues. These are the Instinct for Combinations; Group Persistences or the Persistence of Aggregates; The Need for Expressing Sentiments by External Acts; Residues Connected with Sociality; The Integrity of the Individual and his Appurtenances; and The Sex Residue. [Pareto's classification of the residues is to be found in 1935, II:516–519.] Only two of these classes are of central interest here, namely, the first two, the Instinct for Combinations and Group Persistences. These will serve us to expound Pareto's theory of the circulation of elites.

The instinct for combinations may generally be described as involving combinative and innovative tendencies. Those whom Pareto calls foxes are shrewd, innovative, resourceful, scheming, and quick to adapt themselves. They are disinclined to use force and prefer talk, manipulation, and the use of wily devices. They turn readily to fraud and deception. Foxes are liberally endowed with the sentiments that Class I or combination instincts or residues manifest.

Group persistences, on the other hand, involve anti-innovative or conservative tendencies. Lions stand in contrast with foxes and are endowed with Class II or group-persistence residues. They have a propensity to stay with combinations that already have been made. They are conservative and accordingly adhere to tradition and custom. They are prone to belief in ideals. They are more "faithful" than clever, more believing than skeptical. They are willing to meet opposition head-on and to use force.

Interestingly, although foxes certainly "scheme" and "plan," they do not do so in a long-range fashion. Pareto thought that a predominance of combination instincts and a weakening of group persistences would make a governing class "more satisfied with the present and less thoughtful of the future" [1935, IV:1516].

Pareto associates with the foxes those he calls speculators (or Ss), persons " . . . whose incomes are essentially variable and depend upon . . . wide-awakeness in discovering sources of gain." He associates with the lions those he calls Rentiers (or Rs), " . . . persons who have fixed or virtually fixed incomes not depending to any great extent on ingenious combinations that may be conceived by an active mind" [1935, IV:1561–1562; cf. also IV: 1645–1649]. The logic of this association seems plain enough.

A crucial question for Pareto relates to the distribution or allocation of the residues. How are they distributed as between a governing class or governed elite and those who are governed? The Paretian theory of the elites is ultimately connected with what one might call the arithmetic of the residues.

A "mere handful of citizens" who are willing to employ violence may capture power from public officials who will not meet force with force. If the officials have humanitarian scruples about the use of force, the "handful of citizens" is likely to get its way. But if the officials want to use other devices than force, then there is a good chance that they will resort to the ways of the fox. They will engage in maneuver, trickery, and fraud. The foxes then come to the fore and displace the lions in government.

As the foxes thus displace the lions, the governed class for its part fills up with lions. The foxes of the governing group scheme to deprive the subordinated lions of fox leadership, for they draw the foxes to themselves. They do not have to draw all of those who are endowed with combination instincts to themselves, for some of those with combination instincts are engaged in areas quite outside of politics. Combination instincts in the subject class are often applied to areas and trades having nothing to do with the political arena. This means of course that the problem of maintaining itself is made easier for the governing class. The governing class is in any case much smaller than the class of the governed, and it can change a great deal with the addition to it of relatively small numbers of persons with certain characteristics. For example, relatively small numbers of foxes may considerably enhance its foxlike character.

Although the foxes inevitably maneuver and seek to deprive the "plebeians" below of leadership, still, *in the long run*, if we understand Pareto correctly, they are unlikely to succeed if a strong polarization occurs. Thus, if combination instincts are heavily allocated to the governing class and group persistence instincts heavily allocated to the governed, the governing and governed groups are accordingly polarized between "pure" fox and "pure" lion, or nearly so. At this point there is a real threat of revolution.

The expedients successfully used for a while to stave off revolution are in the end likely to bring it about. The foxes deprive the governed of fox elements. This may bring some temporary advantage to the foxes, but it also works toward an ultimately larger alienation. The same sharp separation of the residues that allows the governing elite to ward off the governed for some time at length brings crisis. The governed will in the end find their leaders and will be disposed to revolt against a governing elite that has lost the will to use force. A new governing class strong in group persistences accordingly aspires to power and, if it succeeds in gaining it, initiates an age of faith rather than of skepticism.

A cyclical pattern is thus suggested, which we may summarize as follows. We begin where we just stopped, with the coming to power of the lions. The lions are willing to use force. But the qualities that win power are not necessarily as good for its maintenance. Force typically gives way to fraud, ruse, and strategem, as the elite seeks to preserve its power. Fox-like skills in diplomacy, finance, and political intrigue may well be called for. The new elite calls back some defeated foxes and allows entree to new foxes. Accordingly, the arithmetic of the residues changes again. The elite becomes filled with Class I residues. Foxes tend to replace lions. But, as already suggested, while the foxes then attempt to hold off the lions who have descended into the governed group and deprive them of their leaders, the subject lions do ultimately tend to revolt. History becomes "a graveyard of aristocracies."

Pareto's account includes many nuances that are not included here. There are many indications that he regards the "ideal" governing elite as having strong infusion of both Class I and Class II residues. Combination instincts can "enrich" the ruling class with individuals who are shrewd and astute. On the other hand, group persistences offer resistance to "harmful inclinations of individual interest" [1935, IV:1556, 1774). Morality and faith in the ruling class may operate to restrain individual interests and impetuous passions. One might say that while combination instincts are an indispensable ingredient for the governing group, they present an "inherently difficult problem of control"—"a problem of keeping the interests in conformity with an ultimate value system" [Parsons 1937, p. 285] Yet group persistences also need balance by combination instincts for a strong elite and lasting political stability to exist.

It is now often complained that Pareto's kind of theory of elites presents numerous difficulties. The contemporary class and elite situation does not have so clear and relatively uncomplicated a form as Pareto contemplated [see, e.g., Meisel 1965, pp. 20–21]. The obvious criticism can be made that Pareto's arithmetic of residue-distribution is a hypothetical arithmetic, not an actual scheme of measurement. One may wonder precisely how Pareto would have regarded the phenomenon of Nazism, with reference, for example, to the really extraordinarily "mixed" character of Hitler, who so strikingly combined traits of the fox and the lion [see Hitler 1939].

It also may be observed that with all of Pareto's knowledge of history his cyclical theory seems peculiarly bloodless, historically speaking. It might well be argued that there are insufficient *particularities* associated with his more "permanent" points of reference—residues or sentiments. How different was ancient Rome from modern Rome or indeed from modern Germany? By Pareto's accounts, the residues (if we may here refer to them as indicative of more permanent points of reference) were evidently pretty much the same two thousand years ago as they are today, and the arithmetic of their distribution would also appear to have been pretty much the same arithmetic. Could Mussolini's march on Rome have occurred in antiquity? Could the Nazi movement have occurred in antiquity also? The questions intimate a curious lack of historical sense in a sociologist who knew a great deal of history. We are suggesting that Pareto's whole scheme calls for a more searching *combined* analysis of both the residues and of the historical circumstances peculiar to different periods than Pareto was able to afford.

Still, history presents the spectacle of "a graveyard of aristocracies." If there was—as indeed there was—a strain of excessive optimism in some of the evolutionary theories, Pareto's cyclical theory, on the other hand, does not offer a particularly cheery vision of the fate of mankind.

Sorokin on Cultural Cycles

This essay deals with "social change," but that concise phrase is not meant to exclude theories with a particular stress on culture—on, say, systems of belief, knowledge, art, law, and so on.

Pitirim A. Sorokin (1889–1968), a Russian-born American sociologist who was a professor at Harvard University, wrote a huge book called *Social and Cultural Dynamics* [1962] in which he did indeed stress culture, although his full title obviously suggests that he did not neglect "society." Sorokin's work is fairly typical of a certain modern genre. It comes close to being "philosophy of history." It is nevertheless also very plainly the product of a sociologist.

The contrast of Sensate, Ideational, and Idealistic types of culture is a well-known contribution of Sorokin's. The two main forms, in his view, are the Sensate and Ideational. The third, the Idealistic, is a fragile kind of combination or synthesis of the other two, likely to be short-lived, even if it is aesthetically more appealing. For Sorokin, the character of the main types depended on premises about "true" or "ultimate" reality. In Sensate culture, such reality is a set of phenomena that can be grasped by the senses. In Ideational culture, "true" or "ultimate" reality transcends the sensible world. Ideational culture is accordingly oriented to postulated things "beyond space and time," and, for it, this sensible, material world is a snare and a delusion, something in any case to be accorded small value by one aware of "true reality."

Sensate culture (at least in what Sorokin called its Active form) makes a direct onslaught on the sensible, material world in order to solve a variety of problems. One might say that it is at its most vigorous and "finest" when its values are carried and exemplified in confrontation of, and action upon, the world by such persons as conquerors of disease, battlers against death, organizers and coordinators of efforts to advance industry and technology. Ideational culture tends to be less concerned with "the world" and more with the inner man. When Sensate values predominate, there might be a great concern with public health (again particularly where we have Active Sensate culture), but Ideational culture might well show a bent toward not being much concerned with health. After all, health is very much a this-worldly good; perhaps it is better not to be overconcerned with it but to strengthen the inner man in a conviction that it is a vain, transitory thing, so that, if it is lost or not gained, little is actually missed.

The foregoing description refers to Active Sensate culture. There are also Passive Sensate and Cynical Sensate culture forms. Passive Sensate culture "sees" the world in terms of means to gain and heighten sensual pleasure. Cynical Sensate culture encourages hypocrisy and facile adaptation to whatever will bring worldly advantage.

Within Ideational culture, Ascetic Ideationalism is a form that thrusts toward making "spiritual" ends all-important, toward minimizing the body, toward maximum detachment from sensible reality. Active Ideationalism maintains sympathy with the Ascetic form but it launches an attack upon the social and cultural world in an effort to push it in the direction of the demands of the spirit. It is oriented to "saving" others as well as oneself. It is constrained to operate within and upon the world since it wants not to be detached from the latter but to transform it.

Active Sensate, Passive Sensate, Cynical Sensate, Active Ideational, and Ascetic Ideational forms, when the intermediate Ideational form is added, yield the six forms that are clearly of some importance to Sorokin. He distinguishes an additional "Pseudo-Ideational form," to which, however, he gives very little space [1962, I:75–76]. The two main Sensate and Ideational forms in the large are the ones that strongly command Sorokin's attention.

Sorokin is clearly interested in the *sequence*, Sensate to Ideational to Idealistic. Since early Greek times, the West, in his view, has completed two cycles of this sequence and is now, for the time, again in a Sensate phase of a third cycle. There are, however, indications, amid contemporary wars and other disastrous phenomena, of a beginning new Ideational (or perhaps Idealistic) culture. The last chapter of the last volume of Sorokin's *Dynamics* is significantly entitled "The Twilight of Our Sensate Culture and Beyond" [1962, IV:775–

779]. We are destined to see a man "still more debased, sensual and material, stripped of anything divine, sacred, and absolute," but beyond the wrath and tears of Sensate decline there "loom the magnificent peaks of the new . . . culture" [1962, IV:775].

Envisioning a post-Sensate culture to come that would be due to put a high value on the "sacred" again, Sorokin anticipated a significant theme in the so-called counter-culture of recent years. To this extent, at least, his cyclical view is not systematically "pessimistic." Moreover, he does not think in terms of an iron sequence and inevitable cyclical recurrence, as we have already indicated. "I nowhere claimed that such an order of succession [Sensate to Ideational to Idealistic] is a universal uniformity. . . . I do not think the sequence observed in the history of the Greco-Roman and the Western cultures is universal or uniform for all societies and at all times" [Sorokin 1964, p. 407]. The repetition of the sequence in the Western world remains real in Sorokin's view, and the cyclical "suggestion" accordingly also remains.

How does change take place from one form to another? Sorokin relies a good deal on the notion of "immanent" change or change that comes from within a cultural scheme or system itself. In this connection he sets out some very dubious ideas, for example the idea that integrated cultural systems change according to a course of life that is "predetermined" by their very nature. The systems are, then, bound to change and they are, as it were, "wound up" so that they are going to change. They are things predestined to decay. This is not of much help. What Sorokin calls the principle of limit is more suggestive. A certain kind of truth will stand just so much emphasis and development before it becomes untruth and distortion, as hammering a piano key harder and harder makes it give forth its distinctive sound that is louder and louder until the key is hammered so hard that it breaks. Cultural systems have a tendency to rise toward a kind of maximum development, too, and then to decline, to become more and more "inadequate." Their "true" parts come to be outweighed by their "false" parts as they cater less and less satisfactorily to the various "needs" of their human carriers.

"Immanent change" is again suggested when Sorokin writes of forms of truth, in particular, as subject to "a self-preparation of their own decline." More fully, he asserts that "all the forms of truth are subject to . . . 'dialectical destiny' and are hardly exempt from a self-preparation of their own decline in the course of their development" [1962, II:121–122]. The notion of immanent change is by no means in itself useless; it must, however, be used with care, sensitivity, and discrimination. (Much change comes in any case from "outside.") But another note is also struck in the brief statement just quoted. When Sorokin becomes concerned more or less forthrightly with "dialectic," he has some provocative things to say about immanent change.

He contends, for example, that there are lines of conduct that arise in connection with the following out of an Ascetic Ideational way that easily lead to the transformation of that way by defeating the detachment from the world that is proper to it. The Ascetic Ideational way can defeat itself out of its own enthusiastic self-extension. Theoretically, when Ascetic Ideationalism seems threatened, one can always draw back and reaffirm detachment from the world, but one is often tempted to do otherwise. Consider what happens when the followers of an Ascetic

Ideational way increase in number. One can theoretically run away from or abandon those followers, but there is frequently a powerful temptation to do otherwise.

The very success of an Ascetic Ideational model or message or image attracts followers. The followers become numerous enough that they must somehow be taught, organized, even disciplined. Organizational needs impose "the world." Ascetic Ideationalism changes to Active Ideationalism.

> When we read about the activities of St. Paul, the great organizer of Christianity, we notice at once . . . how he had to busy himself with worldly matters, and how the empirical world caught him more and more in its web. He had to give instructions to the brethren about this and that, censure them for some things, warn them of others, prohibit some activities, encourage others; and most of the matters in which his flock involved him, from riots and politics to property and wealth, were of this world" [1962, I:136].

The success of Ascetic Ideationalism then leads (by way of the response to the world to which Ascetic Ideationalism often actually is *tempted*) to an involvement with the world that helps to build up an Active rather than Ascetic Ideational form. In this sense, or in line with this tendency, Ascetic Ideationalism carries the seeds of its own decay. A development whereby some form (as a cultural form), in its very reaching out toward success, creates the instrumentalities of its own decline is legitimately called "dialectical."

Sorokin is even suggestive on various *ways* in which a change of the sort just mentioned may take place. Thus, again beginning with the Ascetic context, saints may come to be venerated. They may attract crowds. Let us say they liven up trade. They create a certain prosperity. This, too, may help to bring about a change to Active Ideationalism. In the situation referring to St. Paul, the asceticism of ascetic Christians themselves (although not necessarily that of the particular individual, St. Paul) was apparently affected. In the situation just depicted, the Ascetic form seems rather to be threatened by the chance of reducing asceticism not so much for the saints themselves as for their followers. But again it is the very "success" of saintly asceticism—the success of models who can even be spectacularly ascetic—that has the effect of defeating or diminishing asceticism. There is a dialectical cast to the argument again.

It is most helpful to have suggestions about different dialectical "ways" or "paths" or "mechanisms" whereby particular and important effects are achieved. Much in what we have reviewed in these several paragraphs needs careful scrutiny and refined statement, but it may be argued again that there is value in Sorokin's dialectical bias.

For the rest, his own main categories gave Sorokin much trouble. He himself, no doubt somewhat unhappily, suggested that actual, empirical cultures show a great deal of overlap. Many cultures, at least impressionistically, appear to be *simultaneously* Sensate *and* Ideational or Idealistic. Have there really been the switches, the shifts, the great transitions that Sorokin professed to see, precisely as *he* saw them?

As Sorokin was aware, even the most detached ascetic has to make some concessions to his body if he wants to stay alive. People may "talk" in terms that are unduly suggestive of the prevalence of certain values. As the writer has put the matter elsewhere [Schneider 1968,

147], "Not every discrepancy in cultural styles must be taken with utmost seriousness as a manifestation of fundamental divergence. 'A handmaiden of the Lord,' 'a very fine girl,' and 'quite a kid' may 'mean' much the same, at least in some contexts." Where linguistic styles happen to be considerably influenced by religion, a man may well call his beloved "a handmaiden of the Lord." Where one shies away from the religious style, the beloved may indeed be spoken of in terms having nothing religious about them. Of course, our suggestion is that it is then easy to overlook a great underlying cultural *sameness*. Different ways of saying the same thing are, precisely, different ways of saying the *same* thing. How much cultural "difference" was in the eye of Sorokin himself rather than "actually there," in cultural reality? In our view, Sorokin's greatest weakness is his failure to note how much resemblance there is among different cultures.

This surely does not mean that no cultural-form distinctions can be revealing. It may be taken to imply, however, that such forms have to be described and analyzed with great care. There is the obvious danger, otherwise, of discussing "changes" that have not occurred at all, because inept distinctions have been made (and the danger, too, of failing to record changes because legitimate distinctions have not been made). Sorokin was not the neatest of thinkers, in any case. He could write as if various phenomena simply somehow came out from, "emanated" from basic cultural forms. He was weak on relating culture to varying social circumstances [see Merton 1968, p. 520, and, on emanationism generally, again Weber 1968a, pp. 141–145]. He could argue in rather hopelessly circular fashion about his cultural forms. On the other hand, there is reason to think (or so we have contended) that his dialectic of change is more promising.

A very different strand of classical theory of change is provided as we next take up some ideas offered by Karl Marx. Yet, in a way, it is quite appropriate to have Sorokin and Marx close to one another. Sorokin represents a cultural stress so strong that he can even write at times as if "society" in all its dimensions is merely an outcome (or indeed an "emanation") of culture. This is hardly a Marxian view. Our concern, as was stated in beginning, with regard to the problem-complex of technology-economics on the one hand, and culture on the other, may here be recalled. The heavily cultural preoccupation that Sorokin shows will be encountered, although on quite different terms, in the anthropologist Kroeber, whom we shall consider in due course. (It is to be noted that we refer to a "heavily" cultural preoccupation. Max Weber could hardly be said to be "unconcerned" with cultural phenomena, particularly in view of his great interest in religion. We sometimes must try merely to give rough indications of differences in relative emphasis.)

Conflict, Reason, Religion, and Charisma: Karl Marx and Max Weber

Marxist Thought

Karl Marx (1818–1883) is so widely known that it is unnecessary to describe his career even briefly. Marx's concerns with change and conflict are insistent to the point that almost anything he wrote is likely to feature these realities. Marx always supplied a vivid reminder of the importance of these things in social life. However, it is not a profitable procedure, for those who are interested in forwarding sociology, to package Marxism by itself, as it were, and perhaps label it something like "conflict" sociology and distinguish it from a "consensus" sociology [see Coser 1971, p. 185]. We take it that a sociology that aspires to having anything on the order of scientific value has to take into account both conflict and harmony, both order and disorder, both stability and change. Indeed, a "dialectical" view of social life (which implies insight into how closely connected seeming opposites to one another can be) would appear to require such a stance.

Marx himself, however, was not really interested in sociology as such. We would even go so far as to say that in a way he was not even interested in economics as such. He had important economic views. His technical economic ideas were significant enough to evoke repeated criticisms from scholars of considerable stature. Marx took these ideas seriously. But even here we have to recognize that basic Marxian economic categories often also have a philosophical aspect. (This is missed, for example, in the sharp critique of Marx by Pareto [1965, II:chapter 13]). For all his concern with economics, Marx was above all a critic—of economy and society, to be sure—with a clear revolutionary bent. He was neither a professor nor by primary intent a "scientist" but a political figure with a powerful intellect at work on social science materials for his own political purposes.

There are two main components in Marx's thought to be considered here. For one thing, we shall of course deal with conflict and change; for another, with reason and the outcome of the historical process. We may note just before we turn to these matters that Marx had a side that allies him with evolutionary thought. In addition, a few words about Marxian dialectical outlook may be fitted into our discussion.

Marx had a general interest in economic development and in historical economic types. When he observed, for instance, that ". . . in broad outlines we can designate the Asiatic, the feudal and the modern bourgeois modes of production as so many epochs in the progress of the economic formation of society" [Marx's "Preface" to his

Critique of Political Economy, as quoted by Hobsbawm in Marx 1964, p. 19], we may suspect this sort of interest at once. Marx was much interested in comparing the different modes of exploitation of labor that he conceived to exist under slavery, under feudalism, and under capitalism. Inevitably, his major concern is with "bourgeois society"—or, indeed, modern capitalism. It is this which represents the most highly developed and most highly differentiated historical organization of production [see, e.g., Marx 1973, p. 105]. Capitalism represents the culmination of the evolutionary economic and social development up to Marx's time.

Conflict and Change Under capitalism, the laborer is separated from the means of production. He does not own those means. He brings what Marx calls his labor power to be sold on the market. He applies that labor power, once he is hired by the capitalist, to the means of production and to the materials upon which production works. The laborer, however, is also the untrammeled owner of his own labor power [Marx 1936, I, chapter 6]. He might withhold his labor power, refuse to sell it. Actually, he often has little or no choice and is constrained to sell it. He *is* formally free—even "free" to starve. It is crucial, however, that he does not sell his labor power totally, once and for all. Under capitalism, he has a commodity *to sell* on the market—again, his labor power. He is not a commodity *himself.* Were he to sell his labor power lock, stock, and barrel, once and for all, he would *become* a commodity.

Once the laborer has sold his labor power, he works a certain number of hours per day, for example twelve hours. In Marx's view he will typically produce the value of the goods that are necessary to sustain and maintain him in less than twelve hours, say in nine hours. Then he works three more hours to produce a so-called surplus value that is appropriated by his capitalist employer. The very heart of capitalism is surplus value. It is its life's blood, the indispensable condition for its existence.

The idea of surplus value is bound in with a number of technical economic ideas by Marx. To some of the critics of these ideas, the Marx of the first parts of the third volume of his work, *Capital*, seemed to be abandoning his previous theory of surplus value as set out in the first volume of that work [see particularly the crucial chapter 9 in Marx 1909, III; and the brief discussion in Giddens 1971, pp. 50–52]. We cannot get into this technical detail here. We must be content with the very rough generalization that, *through* the economic detail that Marx discusses, capitalism is represented by him as hurtling to its own doom. (This representation holds at least theoretically, apart from possible empirical modifications.) The Marxian dialectic is at work here and we shall soon say a little more about it.

Capitalism has an industrial reserve, an "army" that is ever ready to be thrown to places in the economy which develop abrupt needs for additional labor power. This army (which has several layers, running down to the most depressed, "stagnant" form, with extremely irregular employment [Marx 1936, I:705]) also serves to keep wages low. The thesis of the increasing misery of the proletariat applies in particular to this industrial reserve army, which expands under capitalism and spreads pauperization.

Economic crises threaten capitalism. The middle class

shrinks, or so one may interpret Marx in the light of his famous thesis that one capitalist kills off many [1936, I:836]—or in the light of the *Communist Manifesto*, with its statement that the lower strata of the middle class ("small tradespeople, shopkeepers, and retired tradesmen generally, the handicraftsmen and peasants") "sink gradually into the proletariat" [Marx & Engels 1932, p. 17]. Something on the order of polarization takes place. Society is riven in two. The conflict due will bring great change. The conditions for revolution now have ripened:

Along with the constantly diminishing number of the magnates of capital . . . grows the mass of misery, oppression, slavery, degradation, exploitation; but with this too grows the revolt of the working-class, a class always increasing in numbers, and disciplined, united, organized by the very mechanism of the process of capitalist production itself. The monopoly of capital becomes a fetter upon the mode of production, which has sprung up along with, and under it. . . . The knell of capitalist private property sounds. The expropriators are expropriated [1936, I:836–837].

The dialectical point involved here may be concisely stated. The surplus value that is the very life's blood of capitalism ultimately becomes the source of its downfall. The expropriators are finally recognized for what they are. It is as if their strength evokes their weakness. There is technical economic development that makes surplus value and profit finally work to the disadvantage of the system that cannot exist without them. In broader terms, the strength of the strong ultimately arouses the ire of the weak. The tensions between the "opposites" of capital and labor within the totality of the old capitalist system finally become unsustainable. It is evident by this point in our review that the theme (with variations) of a system carrying within it the elements that make for its own destruction has been a persistent one in the history of social thought.

It should be added that Marx was aware of the need for numerous qualifications of the views that have been so briefly set out here regarding capitalism and its breakup. There is much in the crucially important first volume of the *Capital* that may be argued, and has been argued, to be "hypothetical." Empirical developments might well modify the theoretical deductions Marx worked out in that volume. In connection with his thesis of pauperization of the working class, Marx wrote of "the absolute general law of capitalist accumulation," but observed that "like all other laws it is modified in its working by many circumstances, the analysis of which does not concern us here" [1936, II:707].

However, the view given in the first volume of *Capital* is one that Marx apparently never entirely relinquished. It remains an important view in his history and development. It clearly features the social conflict and the stress on change we remarked upon in beginning.

Reason and Change The matter of reason and change now requires attention. In recent years there has been renewed interest in Marx among sociologists. There has also been an understandable tendency to write of him in laudatory terms. We say "understandable" because there is a good deal in Marx that constitutes cogent analysis, particularly for and even beyond his time. But along with the laudatory tendency there has also been a tendency to bypass extremely serious questions about Marx's work on certain lines. A generation ago a philosopher like Karl Popper raised such questions more forthrightly than some contemporary sociologists, who are perhaps overconcerned to establish that Marx was "a great man" and overanxious lest dubious elements in his thought be exhibited.

Popper was especially inclined to argue that "history has no meaning" [1950, p. 453]. Popper wanted to deny the notion that "History" is somehow a self-existent phenomenon that has certain things "in mind" for the future. He disputed the notion of a predetermination of history that will make things come out a certain way whether human beings want them to or not. It is as if Popper were challenging a view—and indeed that is how he saw the matter—that "History" has a course all its own, as it were, "above the heads" of human beings.

Marx, as Popper sought to show, is by no means totally free of this view of the historical process. It points to a strain in his thinking, importantly modified by others, but a strain nevertheless. A notion of what this strain is like in Marx is given by Marx's quotation of a Russian reviewer of *Capital*, a quotation that Marx plainly regarded as rendering correctly a significant part of his thought in *Capital*. The review in question asserts:

Marx only troubles himself about one thing; to show, by rigid scientific investigation, the necessity of successive determinate orders of social conditions, and to establish, as impartially as possible, the facts that serve him for fundamental starting points. For this it is quite enough, if he proves at the same time, both the necessity of the present order of things, and the necessity of another order into which the first must inevitably pass over; and this all the same, whether men believe it or do not believe it, whether they are conscious or unconscious of it [Marx 1936, I:22–23].

Now it is true that Marx had a keen sense of how, in human history, purposive social actions have results that are often unintended or unanticipated by the actors themselves. But we see him going beyond this insight. There is a tendency in him to lift the capitalist system beyond human will and human reckoning altogether—toward "the necessity of another order into which the first must inevitably pass over," precisely as in the above quotation. Capitalism hurtles to its own doom because that is the way the Historical Process is loaded, and that is how things will work out, human beings willing or not. This connects with the criticism that Frederick Engels gave of the utopian, the non-"scientific" socialists who had preceded the Marxists.

As Engels put the matter, to the utopian socialists, ". . . society presented nothing but wrongs; to remove these was the task of reason. It was necessary, then, to discover a new and more perfect system of social order and to impose this upon society from without by propaganda, and, wherever it was possible, by the example of model experiments" [1935, p. 36].

Were the utopian socialists not naive? Beyond question, Marx (and Engels) achieved insights into economy and society that the utopian socialists never attained. This, however, is not all that is relevant here. Was it really so foolish to take the view that to remove social wrongs was "the task of reason"? Marx *could* be mistrustful of reason and of a forthright attack on social injustices to the point where he would not rely on so frail a reed as this "reason" seemed to be. Then let reason enter into the Historical Process, into HISTORY. Let *the latter* work out things ultimately in the way that considerations of reason and justice might suggest. Such a course, after all, is safer. To put reason and justice into the Historical Process and to destine the great proletarian class to overcome its oppression via that process is a much more secure thing than to rely on fallible humans trying to better things rationally.

But a price must be paid for this security via the creation of a myth—a myth about history that could indeed be extremely expensive. Seeking to determine what history "had in mind," one might even conclude, as some of the heirs of Marx did, that fascism was "the last stand of the bourgeoisie," a historically necessary interlude before the revolution. To fight against fascism might then even appear counterrevolutionary [Popper 1950, pp. 352–353].

Students of Marxism are well aware that there was another Marx, a Marx who was not at all an historical inevitabilist. This was the Marx who wrote, "Men make their own history." They make *their own* history. The quotation is from a famous tract by Marx and it exhibits neatly the authentic realism that he *could*, indeed, summon. This realism is plainer yet when we put the quotation in its larger original context: "Men make their own history, but they do not make it just as they please; they do not make it under circumstances chosen by themselves, but under circumstances directly encountered, given and transmitted from the past" [Marx n.d., p. 15]. This was the Marx who could see how "tough" and hard to change historically produced circumstances could be, a Marx far removed from utopian naïveté, but at the same time one who saw that no historical spirits or ghosts produced the Historical Process and who might call on human beings *themselves* to pitch in and work to change things.

CONFLICT, REASON, RELIGION, AND CHARISMA   89

It must be insisted again, however, that the historical inevitabilist is there too, within Marx's breast. An able man of letters captured both of the relevant strains in Marx in a passage in which he contended that there is a mythical element, one might say almost a supernatural-determinist element, in Marxism, despite Marx. It is Edmund Wilson who writes:

> It was in vain that Marx tried to bar out Providence: *"History does nothing,"* he had insisted in *The Holy Family;* "it 'possesses *no* colossal riches;' it 'fights no fight.' It is rather *man*—real, living man—who acts, possesses and fights in everything. It is by no means 'History' which uses man as a means to carry out *its* ends, as if it were a person apart; rather History is *nothing* but the activity of man in pursuit of his ends." But as long as he keeps talking as if the proletariat were the chosen instrument of a Dialectic, as if its victory were predetermined, he does assume an extra-human power. . . . There is a non-personal entity called "History" which accomplishes things on its own hook and which will make the human story come out right, no matter what you or your opponent may do [1940, pp. 195–196].

Wilson, too, was aware of the price that had to be paid for this mythical strain in Marx and Marxism. He notes that the German Social Democrats of the Second International, certain that "History" was going to make socialism come about, "were found supporting an imperialist war which was to deprive the working class of all its liberties." Wilson suggests also that the Communists of the Third International "acquiesced in the despotism of Stalin," for the historical process was due to come out right in any case [1940, p. 196]. The agreement with Popper is evident.

A man like the sociologist Hobhouse could have his honest and no doubt very disturbing misgivings about what reason could do about changing the human condition in the direction of the liberal and rational soul's desire. But Hobhouse did not succumb to the illusion that reason secretly makes history run. That illusion can be both politically dangerous and work thorough mischief on any attempt to achieve something on the order of scientific sociological analysis, using the best tools it has and seeking to avoid corruption by ideology and by what ordinarily goes under the name of "wishful thinking." Marx had undeniable powers as an analyst of conflict and change. The inevitabilist-historicist strain in him does not carry forward what those powers otherwise achieved for him.

Weberian Thought

The German sociologist Max Weber (1864–1920) is another towering figure in the history of the field. Afflicted with a serious nervous disorder, Weber was able to do little professorial work, but his may be possibly the most influential career of any sociologist to date.

Much of Weber's thought is centered on modern capitalism, religion, and charisma. Weber was, as we have observed before, considerably influenced by Marx and by the character of the problems Marx posed. But Weber's thought is in no sense a simple derivative from that of Marx. Let us note how Weber's thought emerges in its own vigorous way in the fields of religion and of charisma.

Religion It is well known that Weber made a number of studies in the sociology of religion—*The Protestant Ethic and the Spirit of Capitalism* [1930], *The Religion of*

China [1951], *Ancient Judaism* [1952], and *The Religion of India* [1958] at once occur to the student of Weber, as does the book-length section on religion in *Economy and Society* [1968b, II:399–634]. Much of Weber's thought about religion was concerned with change. Let us consider *The Protestant Ethic* in this connection.

The thesis of *The Protestant Ethic* has been ceaselessly mulled over, interpreted, supported, and disputed. (For a review of some of the older literature on *The Protestant Ethic*, see Biéler [1959, pp. 477–514]; for a concise survey of more recent literature, see Little [1969, pp. 226–237]; for further overall reviews of relevant literature, see Schneider [1970, chapter 6]; and Nelson, in Glock and Hammond [1973, chapter 2].) It is not altogether easy to state Weber's thesis briefly. He did think that there were close connections between the Protestant ethic and the antitraditionalist spirit of modern capitalism. Modern capitalism does not seek to limit economic enterprise by traditional needs, which, once satisfied, call forth no more economic effort. Modern capitalism, further, seeks to conduct enterprise with disciplined ways of work and with maximum technological and financial rationality.

The crucial Calvinist ethic, in particular, set forth a doctrine of predestination according to which some human beings were saved and some reprobated or damned, according to the pleasure of an inscrutable God, while in principle no one could say who would be saved and who would not. In the anxiety that this sort of doctrine aroused in an age in which salvation seemed all-important, Protestant pastors who adhered to the doctrine advised that their parishioners must fight any doubts about salvation as inspired by the demon and, additionally, engage in hard, methodical work within the world. It was well indeed to be ascetic. (The world was made for God, in any case, and not for man or his pleasures or happiness.) But the asceticism must be an asceticism within the world, not the asceticism of monastic removal from the world. Calvinism had an important share in providing a disciplined, reliable labor force, released from traditional limitations on the amount of work a man might undertake to do occasioned by his working to attain only an established standard of living. Hard work was valued both by Calvinist (or Pietist or Methodist or Baptist) workmen and by their employers of the same religious persuasion.

Roads to enhanced productivity were thus opened up, Weber suggested. Since the branches of ascetic Protestantism just mentioned also encouraged negative attitudes toward cultural expenditures and toward "idle pleasures," a certain accumulation of capital was also likely to occur. "Protestant virtues" of industry, thrift, and frugality, however, as they led to worldly wealth, also helped along a development whereby the original notion that one could not tell whether a person was going to be saved or not was modified. One significant line of thought became that one could tell from a man's worldly condition, his possession or nonpossession of wealth, whether he was genuinely among the saved. Also, accumulated wealth sometimes created irresistible temptations to which some of the Protestant brethren succumbed. Their very virtues of industry, thrift, and frugality produced income and worldly goods that seduced them into losing those same virtues.

Weber was hardly naïve about how ideas and values take their effect. He knew they do not operate in a social or economic or political vacuum. Calvinism did not create modern capitalism sheerly out of its own essence or by virtue of a kind of emanation from itself. Yet Weber did evidently mean to allow some force, in the change to modern capitalism in the West, to religious ideas and values, as well as to religious interests, for the interest in salvation is, precisely, a religious interest. Even if it is agreed that the Protestant ethic provided some sort of scaffolding for the building of modern capitalism, the scaffolding has long since been removed and the building now stands by itself, independent of any sort of religious support or religious adjunct or aid. Modern capitalism itself has been characterized, once more, by a disciplined labor force that can without undue difficulty be induced to work well beyond, for example, the hours required merely to get enough to sustain a traditional standard of living. It has further been characterized by the separation of business from the household and by rational book-keeping.

The Protestant ethic now suggests "disciplined," responsible attitudes toward the materials with which one works. It suggests responsibility toward the job itself. It suggests control of impulses at least sufficient to inhibit such things as coming to the job drunk—or, one might say today, in the light of countercultural phenomena of the nineteen-sixties, under the influence of drugs. The ethic carries its suggestions with respect to entrepreneurs as well as with respect to workers.

How *much* Protestant ethic is now actually left over residually in connection with *production*? Can a modern kind of economic enterprise be carried on at all without a substantial Protestant ethic component—of values that encourage responsibility toward job, machines, materials worked with, and so on? There are significant questions as to the extent to which the Protestant ethic has declined or decayed in the sphere of *consumption*, where ascetic inhibitions appear to have weakened very greatly in Western societies [cf. Bell 1973].

Dispute about the Protestant ethic will undoubtedly go on. Some of the considerable pertinent literature may well cease to indicate profitable lines of inquiry. How much may be gained from still more studies seeking to probe differences (that are somehow seemingly relevant to Weber's Protestant ethic thesis) between American Catholics and American Protestants today? There are other studies suggested by Weber's work that would allow rather rich enterprises in a historical sociology of religion that have perhaps not yet been so well or so fully done as they might be. For instance, there are the various developments that doctrines about "signs" of salvation have gone through that seem to merit further exploration than they have received to date. There are fascinating possibilities in the way of studying how the Protestant ethic came to be "mentalized"—how it came about that prosperity came to be connected in American cultist thought with the idea, for instance, that prosperity argues or implies, not salvation in the older sense, but positive thinking, while poverty argues negative or wrong thinking [Schneider 1970, pp. 115–117; Schneider & Dornbusch, 1958, pp. 101–105]. The mentalization of the Protestant ethic, as far as the indications, for example, of this writer's work go, is definitely connected with changing economic and business circumstances in America.

Since Weber's day other questions suggested by the Protestant ethic have been extended to the world beyond the West. What is needed to "modernize" a nonmodern country? Can one sensibly look for "modernizing" resources in various non-Western religions or can one not? (On this too there is a sizable literature: see for example, Bellah [1957]; McClelland [1961, chapter 9]; Singer [1972, part IV].) How can both workers and entrepreneurs be "modernized"?

Even in the Western world, as, for example, E. P. Thompson's massive work [1964] on the English workingclass shows, and as we have already noted, the emergence of industrial factory discipline was not an easy, automatic thing. Russia, Japan, China, and other countries have all had their struggles with this. In Madras in India, Singer discerned a "Hindu ethic" that clearly involves devotion to work in modern industrial and business contexts, and which he studied as it manifested itself among a number of industrial leaders. Singer contended that Weber was wrong on much relating to India and the background of the Hindu religion. Yet it is significant that he thinks the "Hindu ethic" energizes work in the industrial-business context and allows Indian businessmen to feel that in their devotion to business and industry they are being good men of religion, not merely businessmen.

Some scholars would find the various matters relating to modernization, which we have so barely indicated, only slightly if at all illuminated by Weber's work. But Weber's effective stimulation in these matters is beyond question. Rather than agitate about the "credit" due or not due to him in this connection, just now it is more profitable to refer to a major problem relating to social and cultural change that his work in the sociology of religion generally raised. It is a most tenacious and most difficult problem, at least in the terms in which it has usually been put.

In his recent provocative volume, *Weber and Islam,* Bryan Turner, following Alasdair MacIntyre, suggests that ". . . in attempting to explain the relationship between beliefs and actions, sociologists have often started with a strong thesis and ended with a compromise." Turner continues: "The strong thesis is either that beliefs are secondary (Marx and Pareto) or that beliefs are independent and influential (Weber). Most sociologists finish by eating their own words" [1974, p. 9]. The point of this of course has to do with just what Weber contended for in *The Protestant Ethic.* Did Weber eat his own words? Did he so modify a thesis about the influence of (religious) ideas, values and interests on economic life that in the end his position was practically Marxian? It is well to recall that Marx could write flatly that "the religious world is *but* the reflex of the real world" [Marx 1936, I:91; italics supplied]. (We *interpret* Marx here as setting out a highly "materialistic" view of religion. [Note the whole passage from which we draw in Marx 1936, I:91–92.]) It is hard to imagine Weber writing this. It may be suggested that a significant contrast *does* remain between Marx and Weber. With all of Weber's awareness of how "spiritual" and "material" factors may interact, and with all other statements by Marx indicating he was no crude materialist that one may wish to adduce, Weber and Marx are still not the same: they do not see the "spiritual" and the "material" in the same way or as having the same efficacy. (Of course the whole matter is particularly relevant to the ways of change.) However one finally construes Weber's meaning in *The Protestant Ethic,* it would clearly do violence to that meaning to take it as indicating that "the religious world is *but* the reflex of the real world."

Again, textual comparison of Marx and Weber on

these matters would not yield simple, perfectly obvious, perfectly straightforward results. Still more important, however, in the whole matter of assessing change, we are far from knowing how "properly" to assess the force and relevance of "spiritual" and "material" factors. There are a few things we can say or do with confidence. We can, for example, well avoid the naïveté of emanationism. But for the purposes of solid analysis in these spheres, we still have very much to learn. There are controversies about the relative significance of the "spiritual" and "material" that we simply cannot (now, at any rate) settle: we lack the analytical resources and we often lack relevant evidence.

Charisma Another main line of Weber's thought relative to change is rendered by his notion of charisma. He distinguished three pure types of authority—legal authority, "resting on a belief in the legality of enacted rules"; traditional authority, "resting on an established belief in the sanctity of immemorial traditions and the legitimacy of those exercising authority under them"; and lastly, charismatic authority, "resting on devotion to the sanctity, heroism or exemplary character of an individual person, and of the normative patterns or order revealed or ordained by him . . ." [1968b, I:215].

Certainly, Weber was interested in noncharismatic bases of authority, but charisma was also clearly of much interest for him. He originally defined charisma as a quality of an individual that causes him to be considered extraordinary, either in virtue of his supposed supernatural character or endowments, or in virtue of exceptional attributes or powers imputed to him. But Weber also allowed that charisma could attach to an office or an institution. The office of the Catholic priest has for many centuries been regarded within the church as having charismatic or sacred quality. The priest who administers the sacraments may be corrupt or depraved, but this does not mitigate or impair the sacred value of the sacramental performances in which he engages. The corruption of the "vessel," in this case, in no way affects the quality of the "liquid" it contains. Charisma inheres in the priestly office.

Weber finds charisma characteristic for "prophetic movements" and "expansive political movements in their early stages," but, he adds, where domination is once well established, "and above all as soon as control over large masses of people exists, it gives way to the forces of everyday routine" [1968b, I:252]. The "routinization of charisma" has become a famous phrase among sociologists. (It is worth noting that the German word Weber utilized that is translated as routinization is *"Veralltäglichung,"* which literally means "every-day-ization," or making into an everyday phenomenon or thing.) The idea is that of reducing something to the usual, almost the humdrum, taking out of it the exceptional or "magical" or the very "exciting."

Routinization comes about as, for example, a great founder figure of religion who evokes a tremendous emotional response gives way to organizers and church bureaucrats who institute discipline and rules for the masses who may have been attracted by the founder in the first place. We previously quoted Sorokin on the subject of St. Paul, "the great organizer of Christianity," who had to "busy himself with worldly matters" and was more and more entangled in the web of the world.

Sorokin here begins to point to what Weber meant by the routinization of charisma. The "great organizer" indeed gets an organization going. The organization "contains" the masses who belong to it, who are in some sense disciplined and ruled by it.

Weber writes that "domination congeals into a permanent structure." The entire sentence in which this phrase appears reads thus: "As domination congeals into a permanent structure, charisma recedes as a creative force and erupts only in short-lived mass emotions with unpredictable effect . . ." [1968, III:1146].

Perhaps it is not unduly misleading to say that (as Weber sees matters) charisma is subject to a kind of entropy, to a kind of degeneration or attenuation, as the process of routinization takes place. But when charisma does "come to life," it can be an extremely powerful force. It has been possessed of course by religious leaders but it may also be possessed by political leaders, as already intimated, by military men, and presumably even by college professors. Clara Bow, a famous movie actress of an earlier day, was said to possess "It." Exactly what "It" was no one seemed quite certain, but that was even part of its charm and power. Given its connection with the beauteous Clara Bow, "It" did clearly have a sexual connotation. Charisma might be defined as a sort of generalized "It," without any necessary sexual reference. Weber was interested in its transformative power, on the one hand, and in its routinization on the other.

Because of his very considerable historical knowledge, Weber was able to give a provocative analysis of charisma and its routinization. But his analysis still did not carry very far, and possibly he never intended to give more than the sketches of charisma and its routinization that he did give.

Let us allude to routinization again. Weber wrote that "... it is the fate of charisma to recede before the powers of tradition or of rational association after it has entered the permanent structures of social action," adding that "this waning of charisma generally indicates the diminishing importance of individual action" [1968b, III:1148–1149]. The heroic and ecstatic become tame; excitement, mania, and tremendous fervor are toned down. They get put in boxes, so to speak—like the box of a church organization. Is this a straightforward, necessarily continuous "decline"? Or, at any rate, a "decline" only halted briefly, now and then, by "short-lived mass emotions with unpredictable effect," in words of Weber's that have been quoted already? As charisma is thinned or attenuated, as the "spirit" becomes pale, is it nevertheless more inflammable in some places, in some social loci, than in others? These are questions of obvious interest. Weber might well have said *more* than he said or implied about the prospects and "fate" of charisma in a bureaucratic world.

Weber's views on charisma have been criticized, notably by Edward Shils, who finds Weber's very distinction of legal, traditional, and charismatic types of authority overly rigid. Shils argues that Weber failed to see, or at least failed to make clear, that an element of the charismatic attaches *also* to legal and traditional forms of authority. These forms, too, have something of the extraordinary, the noneveryday imputed to them. Weber was right, as Shils says, to note the scope and force of "processes of rationalization and bureaucratization"

[1975, p. 261] in modern society. Nevertheless, this does not justify a view of modern society as being historically unique in that charisma constantly diminishes within it (if we interpret Weber as asserting this, as there is reason for doing).

Shil's criticisms are well conceived and rest on a view of the role of charisma in societies at large which his book, *Center and Periphery,* seeks to give strong support. If Shils is right, the view of change we hold must obviously be affected. If charisma has had more force in modern society than Weber allowed, that has consequences for our view of its character in relation to other societies. If, as Shils also contends, charismatic quality even attaches to classes within modern mass society that were previously effectively outside charismatic range, that suggests *other* changes that need our consideration. [For another criticism of Weber on charisma, see Stark 1970, IV.]

Enough has been said about Weber's views of charisma, however, to suggest once more that he makes an effective contrast figure to Marx. Just as it is hard to get away from the implications of Marx's flat statement that the religious world is but the reflex of the real world, and from a significant contrast between Marx and Weber that this already intimates, so it is hard to relinquish the impression that charisma would not have been of much interest to Marx. Marx sought the sources of change in hard economic realities (or what he took to be such), in the consequences of exploitation, in the polarization of society, in the swallowing of one capitalist by many, in the escalating misery of the industrial reserve army. Weber lived in a more "social" world where bureaucracies and a variety of other social structures loom large but where the routine of structure can be broken, even if rarely and sporadically, by outbursts occasioned by powerful, moving messages from figures who are extraordinary or are considered supernatural. Marx was not unaware of "society" or of man's sheer humanity and personal qualities, nor was Weber casual about the economic aspects of societies. There is nevertheless a difference of emphasis that draws the attention of one man (Marx) toward *economy*-and-society and the attention of the other (Weber) toward economy-and-*society*. Sociology clearly needs both kinds of emphasis.

Notes on Technology and Culture: William F. Ogburn and Alfred L. Kroeber

Marx and Weber pose for us the gigantic problem of the relative roles of "ideas" and of "economic" factors in change. This essay cannot even help improve the statement of the problem. It is sufficient to thrust it insistently upon the reader's attention. In this section, the problem is again suggested because we put together a view of change that stresses technology and one that concentrates on culture.

Two recent writers engage us here, the sociologist William F. Ogburn and the anthropologist Alfred L. Kroeber. Ogburn, to whom we turn first, lacks the stature of most of the men we have considered, but his work calls for brief notice because of his view of cultural lag.

Ogburn on Cultural Lag

William F. Ogburn (1886–1959) taught sociology at Columbia University and at the University of Chicago.

He had a great interest in social statistics and developed a concept of cultural lag that is still referred to and utilized.

"Theory" seems a particularly portentous word to use for Ogburn's concept of cultural lag. Ogburn nevertheless presents the germ of a significant idea when he writes of this phenomenon. The "theory," then, has to do with Ogburn's perception of a problem of "adjustment between the different parts of culture," as he puts the matter in his *Social Change* [1922, p. 200]. He introduces his thesis with respect to cultural lag as follows:

The thesis is that the various parts of modern culture are not changing at the same rate, some parts are changing much more rapidly than others; and that since there is a correlation and interdependence of parts, a rapid change in one part of our culture requires readjustments through other changes in the various correlated parts of culture. . . . Where one part of culture changes first, through some discovery or invention, and occasions changes in some part of culture dependent upon it, there frequently is a delay in the changes occasioned in the dependent part of culture. The extent of this lag will vary according to the nature of the cultural material, but may exist for a considerable number of years, during which time there may be said to be a maladjustment [1922, pp. 200–201].

The notion of cultural lag that Ogburn advances comes to rely on a distinction between material and nonmaterial culture. Material culture comprises such items as "houses, factories, machines, raw materials, manufactured products, foodstuffs and other material objects" [1922, p. 202]. Nonmaterial culture includes such phenomena as "customs," "folkways," "social institutions," "beliefs," "philosophies," "laws," and "governments." There is a strategic portion of this nonmaterial culture "which is adjusted or adapted to the material conditions" [1922, p. 203]. This, then, is the central point: "When the material conditions change, changes are occasioned in the adaptive culture. But these changes in the adaptive culture do not synchronize exactly with the change in the material culture. There is a lag which may last for varying lengths of time, sometimes, indeed, for many years" [1922, p. 203].

Ogburn is loose in working out his basic views. His idea of material culture affords an example of this looseness. Sometimes material culture seems to refer somewhat vaguely to "material conditions"; sometimes to cultural "embodiments" in concrete objects, such as the aforementioned houses, factories, machines, and so on. Ogburn notes that there was a time in the United States when people worked "exploitatively" in relation to forests, hewing them down and utilizing timber as they pleased. The American forests were already in process of being destroyed when it became evident that they would soon be inadequate for the needs of the people. Ogburn observes that accordingly a new adaptive culture, one of conservation, thereby became "suited to the material conditions." If cultural lag means that one item of culture moves ahead or changes while another, related item lags behind, then it is at least not clarifying to switch suddenly from "material culture" to "material conditions," as if they were the same. In the example of the forests, it would seem that orientations to nature—"values"—appropriate (that is, not unduly damaging to people's interests) at one time are not appropriate at another time, under changed conditions of population increase, already-effected destruction of forests, and so on.

A certain minimum care and tidiness in a sociologist's

language can hardly do harm. One might consider that if machinery is utilized in a kind of easygoing way at one time and few industrial accidents occur, while it is utilized in a much less easygoing way at another time to the accompaniment of a much higher incidence of industrial accidents, Ogburn would again speak of cultural lag and certain problems would again arise. "Material culture" would not have changed in this example. The *machinery* would be quite the same, but its utilization would be governed by certain standards or goals at one time; by different ones, at a later time. The "lag" in, say, adequate workmen's compensation laws would not be a lag between "material" and "non-material" culture. If we are going to think in theoretical terms at all, it is obviously well to do so with a certain discipline.

Ogburn stimulated thought about change and his research on technology as a change-making agent was certainly stimulating. (His work on independent invention was also provocative: see, for example, Merton [1973, chapter 16].) The concept of cultural lag, however, does not finally carry us beyond a certain level of description that applies to some phenomena. There is of course no reason why change must "start" in the "material culture" (or "material conditions") area, although, obviously, in a society with a highly dynamic technology, it frequently does.

But it might be the other way around. Lag could be occasioned because of change in "nonmaterial" culture, while "material culture" was in some sense constrained to catch up. Thus, Smelser refers to African societies where great new programs of education are being launched prior to large economic growth. In these cases, ". . . educational advances are putting pressure on the societies to develop their economies so that the educated and trained personnel may be absorbed." Smelser adds that then ". . . these societies may be described as experiencing a lag, but the lag is just the reverse of that postulated by Ogburn" [1973, p. 738]. In this context it is well to recall that Max Weber sought to show the influence for change exercised by religious ideas, values, and interests. This concern of Weber's does not constitute a criticism of Ogburn, but it may serve to suggest that, from the point of view of a wide-ranging historical and comparative sociology, the kind of preoccupation with change that Ogburn showed has its sharp limitations and could hardly of itself lead to a well-developed general theory of change.

Kroeber on Culture Growth

Alfred L. Kroeber (1876–1960) was a professor of anthropology at the University of California at Berkeley. He contributed to a variety of areas within his field and is well known as a theorist of culture.

Kroeber's wide-ranging and painstaking work entitled *Configurations of Culture Growth* [1944] appeared at the very end of the period we have considered and again turns our attention to cultural phenomena in particular. Kroeber's thesis in this book is that great achievements (where indeed they occur) in realms such as science, philosophy, literature, and the various arts come in clusters. The possibilities of certain forms or styles are worked out. Those who come relatively late in the development of a cultural cluster may find that most of the possibilities are already exhausted. A certain mode of philosophizing, say, presents a variety of problems. Within some limited time, the mode or style is more or less "finished." The obvious and even the less obvious questions it suggests are taken up and answered—perhaps as well as they ever can be. By way of example, a Scottish outburst in philosophy took up a good part of the eighteenth century but was substantially "finished" by the end of the first quarter or first third of the nineteenth century.

Even persons of great genius who come along "late" may not achieve a great deal because the various developments allowed by a given mode, style, form, or pattern have already been exploited. Men are then often driven to new expedients and a cultural form, pattern, or style may become "disorganized" or "disintegrated" as they try to achieve something novel and distinctive. However, efforts also may be made to "freeze" achieved solutions of cultural problems for long periods.

Kroeber is very cautious and carefully follows the movement of such data as he has. If the conclusions to which he can come are only modest, he is quite willing that this modesty be evident. He shows an unpretentious skepticism with regard to various ambitious theories of culture and history. He sees little or nothing that is "necessary" in cultural developments. Thus, he remarks, "There is nothing to show either that every culture must develop patterns within which a florescence of quality is possible, or that, having once so flowered it withers without chance of revival" [1944, p. 761]. Kroeber is characteristically dubious about the notion that Western culture is necessarily in "decline." [See also in this connection chapter 49, "Is Western Civilization Disintegrating or Reconstituting?" in Kroeber 1952.]

There are those who would criticize Kroeber for being

too disinclined to attempt to construct something like systematic theories of culture and cultural change. His skepticism, his great knowledge, and his good sense are all fine qualities, these critics might argue, but could we not have more on theoretical lines? Perhaps it is inevitable that Kroeber, given his cautious intellectual temperament, should be unable to satisfy such critics. In any case, he hardly takes his fundamental ideas beyond the level of common sense. Thus, he is incessantly concerned with "pattern." The following sentences are indicative of the mode of his discourse on pattern.

The reason for the transience of high-value patterns is not altogether clear. It is evident that such patterns must be selective and somehow differentiated or specialized. This in turn necessitates that any such pattern early takes a particular direction. The pattern is then gradually pushed to its limits in that direction. . . . The very selection which at the outset is necessary if a distinctive pattern is to be produced is almost certain later to become a limitation. It is then often or normally too late to go back to widen the scope of the pattern without undoing the entire growth which it has achieved. It seems to be historically almost as difficult to reconstitute a pattern fundamentally, or to widen greatly the scope of a growth, as at an earlier stage it is difficult to get a distinctive pattern growth or pattern value started. Not infrequently, when a pattern has attained realization or reached saturation, its limitations appear to be felt and efforts are made to alter or enlarge it. If these efforts take the form of a pause in activity, there may be a reconstitution of energy and direction, with the result that, after a lull, growth is resumed along somewhat new and broader lines. The early eighteenth-century pause in the growth of European science is an illustration of this type of phenomenon [1944, p. 840].

This is the Kroeberian style—if one will, it is Kroeber's own "pattern." "Pattern" is obviously not a notion far from common sense. This is true also of "pattern saturation," which means simply that the patterns or forms of a culture develop to the limits of their potentialities and then "pressures" arise so that the patterns are likely to be changed, or dissolved, or expanded; or else there will be a tendency toward repetition and something on the order of "retrogression" [1944, pp. 320, 666].

Consider "Byzantinism," another interesting term not Kroeber's own, but one that he uses and that is quite relevant to his concerns. Suppose there has been what Kroeber calls a peak of pattern realization. The pattern has realized its highest potential. The poetry or music, for example, that features the pattern has become as exquisite or moving as it can be. Then, Kroeber says, one sees endeavors that put "strain" on the pattern. It threatens to "rupture." Impulses toward change may sometimes take the form of "extravagance, flamboyance, or alteration for the sake of novelty." At other times such impulses are repressed and any kind of important change is found intolerable. Accordingly, there is no outlet for activity other than ". . . essential repetition, which necessarily brings with it deterioration of quality. This is the condition familiar as Byzantinism" [1944, pp. 840–841].

Kroeber's language is both commonsense language and metaphorical language. He has a great deal to say that is most interesting, in historical and comparative terms, on the subject of cultural change and stability. His book on configurations [1944] is a monument of learning. It still relies on conceptual units—pattern, pattern saturation, Byzantinism—that do not seem very promising for the purposes of building an ambitious or systematic theory of cultural change. A later work of Kroeber's, the great second edition of his *Anthropology* [1948], although it is barely outside our time span, is worth a word. This volume had more rather commonsense concepts to add and presented more—and sometimes excellent—historical and comparative material on culture. However, in theoretical impressiveness it did not much surpass the earlier *Configurations*.

Looking back to such huge endeavors in analysis of cultural change as Sorokin's *Dynamics*. Kroeber's *Configurations* (and parts of his *Anthropology* of 1948), or Spengler's *Decline of the West* (which we have not considered in this essay), one may often be impressed by the sweep and energy of these writers. But the study of cultural change in them has clearly (as Kroeber was indeed aware) not come upon strategic units of analysis, such as "atoms," "genes," or even "phonemes" or "morphemes" [see Kroeber & Kluckhohn n.d., p. 319]. It is also, incidentally, a question whether there has been any real improvement in this respect since their day. Here, too, there is a difficult area of work.

Concluding
Remarks

As was indicated in the beginning, a certain arbitrariness in choice of theorists has been inevitable. Many names—including some important ones—have had to be omitted. The foregoing pages nevertheless constitute a survey of representative thought of the kind with which this essay is concerned. It has been intended, of course, to emphasize certain points. These are not necessarily always the points that were primary in the minds of the theorists reviewed. There are intellectual historians today who see little merit in stressing ideas that were not present to the minds of those whose work they consider. Karl Marx presumably did not have it in mind to contribute to sociology. He did so nevertheless, and, from our point of view, *that* is important too. We would disagree with those historians inclined to be alert only to the subjective point of view of the historical actor. The effects of the thought of that actor, whether foreseen or contemplated by him or *not,* demand attention too.

The concerns that have been stressed relating to dialectic, the role of reason in change, and the "proper" array or arrangement of technology-economics and culture for purposes of an ambitious theory of change were to a considerable extent "in the consciousness" of the men we have considered. But not all the matters we have touched on were present to the minds of all of them or to an equal extent for all of them. Our three concerns have been chosen partly with an eye to present-day problems in sociology.

We can only suggest once more that dialectical approaches to change may be most fruitful. There are metaphors about "success" leading to "failure" or "failure" to "success," ideas about the tension of opposites within a systemic setup, and other dialectical notions that may lend themselves to close, rigorous scrutiny and generate challenging hypotheses about change. This obviously points to matter that goes beyond purely historical interest.

While the concern with the role of reason in change may in some ways appear peculiarly "philosophical," it is very far from being irrelevant to the concerns of the present-day sociologist. Ideas about the role of reason in change can be most revealing about "what we really think" about the social order, what we conceive it to be "like." This whole matter, too, is worth the closest scrutiny.

The last, huge concern about technology-economics and culture represents a problem or set of problems that is without doubt disconcertingly huge. It is still hard to get away from it if sociologists aspire to comprehensive comparative understanding of macro change. As we have suggested, its very wording must be carefully watched. It may in time break down into a number of more sharply stated and conceived problems. It imposes itself on one repeatedly as one reviews classical theories of change. Thinkers as diverse and of as varying stature as Sorokin and Marx and Weber and Ogburn thrust it at us. In one way or another, present-day sociology has to engage with it.

The classical theorists of course could not foresee the precise character of present-day sociological thought. This does not make them flatly "irrelevant." True, it would be foolish to idolize "ephemeral persons" or "ephemeral systems," in Toynbee's language. Indeed, we have sought to state such merits as the classical theorists may have with due restraint. It is to be hoped, however, that this essay will reinforce the notion that it would also be unwise to allow the heritage of thought about change that has been only too briefly and selectively reviewed here to slip away from us.

Bibliography

W. Bagehot, *Physics and Politics*. Knopf, 1948.

D. Bell, *The Coming of Post-Industrial Society*. Basic Books, 1973.

R. N. Bellah, *Tokugawa Religion*. The Free Press, 1957.

A. Biéler, *La Pensée Economique et Sociale de Calvin*. Geneva: Librairie de l'Université, 1959.

A. Comte, *The Positive Philosophy,* 2 vols. London: Chapman, 1853.

A. Comte, *System of Positive Polity*. London: Longmans Green. Vol. II, 1875. Vol. III, 1876. Vol. IV, 1877.

L. A. Coser, *Masters of Sociological Thought*. Harcourt Brace Jovanovich, 1971.

C. Darwin, *The Origin of Species* and *The Descent of Man*. Modern Library, 1936.

E. Durkheim, *The Division of Labor in Society*. Macmillan, 1933.

E. Durkheim, *Socialism*. Antioch Press, 1958.

F. Engels, *Socialism, Utopian and Scientific*. International Publishers, 1935.

F. Engels, *The Origin of the Family, Private Property, and the State*. International Publishers, 1942.

A. Ferguson, *The History of the Progress and Termination of the Roman Republic*. London: Jones and Co., 1825.

A. Ferguson, *An Essay on the History of Civil Society*. Edinburgh: The University Press, 1966.

J. G. Frazer, *The Golden Bough*, 1-vol. ed. Macmillan, 1958.

A. Gerschenkron, *Economic Backwardness in Historical Perspective*. Harvard University Press, 1962.

A. Gerschenkron, *Continuity in History and Other Essays*. Harvard University Press, 1968.

A. Giddens, *Capitalism and Modern Social Theory*. London: Cambridge University Press, 1971.

C. Y. Glock and P. E. Hammond, *Beyond the Classics?* Harper, 1973.

A. A. Goldenweiser, *Early Civilization*. Knopf, 1922.

A. M. Greeley, *Why Can't They Be Like Us?* Dutton, 1971.

G. Heard, *The Source of Civilization*. London: Cape, 1935.

A. Hitler, *Mein Kampf*. Reynal and Hitchcock, 1941.

L. T. Hobhouse, *Social Development*. Holt, 1924.

L. T. Hobhouse, *Morals in Evolution*. Holt, 1929.

L. T. Hobhouse, G. C. Wheeler, and M. Ginsberg, *The Material Culture and Social Institutions of the Simpler Peoples*. Humanities Press, 1965.

A. L. Kroeber, *Configurations of Culture Growth*. University of California Press, 1944.

A. L. Kroeber, *Anthropology*. Harcourt, Brace, 1948.

A. L. Kroeber, *The Nature of Culture*. University of Chicago Press, 1952.

A. L. Kroeber and C. Kluckhohn, *Culture: A Critical Review of Concepts and Definitions*. Random House, n.d.

W. C. Lehmann, *Adam Ferguson and the Beginnings of Modern Sociology*. Columbia University Press, 1930.

G. and J. Lenski, *Human Societies*. McGraw-Hill, 1974.

D. Little, *Religion, Order, and Law*. Harper & Row, 1969.

J. Lopreato, ed., *Vilfredo Pareto*. Crowell, 1965.

J. Lopreato, *The Sociology of Vilfredo Pareto*. General Learning Press, 1975.

S. Lukes, *Emile Durkheim*. Harper & Row, 1972.

H. S. Maine, *Ancient Law*. London: Oxford University Press, 1959.

M. Mandelbaum, *History, Man, and Reason.* Johns Hopkins Press, 1971.

K. Marx, *Capital.* Vol. I, Modern Library, 1936. Vol. III, Kerr, 1909.

K. Marx, *Pre-Capitalist Economic Formations.* London: Lawrence and Wishart, 1964.

K. Marx, *Grundrisse.* Vintage Books, 1973.

K. Marx, *The Eighteenth Brumaire of Louis Bonaparte.* Moscow: Foreign Language Publishing House, n.d.

K. Marx and F. Engels, *The Communist Manifesto.* International Publishers, 1932.

D. C. McClelland, *The Achieving Society.* Van Nostrand, 1961.

J. H. Meisel, ed., *Pareto and Mosca.* Prentice-Hall, 1965.

R. K. Merton, "Durkheim's Division of Labor in Society." *American Journal of Sociology*, 1934, 40:319–328.

R. K. Merton, *Social Theory and Social Structure.* Free Press, 1968.

R. K. Merton, *The Sociology of Science.* University of Chicago Press, 1973.

J. Millar, *An Historical View of the English Government*, 4 vols. London: Mawman, 1803.

L. H. Morgan, *Ancient Society.* Harvard University Press, 1964.

T. Munro, *Evolution in the Arts.* Cleveland Museum of Art, 1963.

B. Nelson, "Weber's Protestant Ethic: Its Origins, Wanderings and Foreseeable Futures." In C. Y. Glock and P. E. Hammond, eds., *Beyond the Classics?* Harper & Row, 1973.

R. A. Nisbet, *Social Change and History.* Oxford University Press, 1969.

R. A. Nisbet, *The Sociology of Émile Durkheim.* Oxford University Press, 1974.

W. F. Ogburn. *Social Change.* B. W. Huebsch, 1922.

V. Pareto, *The Mind and Society*, 4 vols. Harcourt, Brace, 1935.

V. Pareto, *Les Systèmes Socialistes,* 2 vols. Geneva: Libraire Droz, 1965.

T. Parsons, *The Structure of Social Action.* McGraw-Hill, 1937.

T. Parsons, *Societies: Evolutionary and Comparative Perspectives.* Prentice-Hall, 1966.

T. Parsons, "Vilfredo Pareto: Contributions to Sociology." In *International Encyclopedia of the Social Sciences.* Macmillan and The Free Press, 1968, XI:411–415.

K. R. Popper, *The Open Society and its Enemies.* Princeton University Press, 1950.

L. Schneider, "Pitirim A. Sorokin: Social Science in the

Grand Manner." *Social Science Quarterly,* 1968, 49:142–151.

L. Schneider, *Sociological Approach to Religion.* Wiley, 1970.

L. Schneider, "Tension in the Thought of John Millar." *Studies in Burke and His Time,* 1971–72, XIII: 2083–2098.

L. Schneider and S. M. Dornbusch, *Popular Religion.* University of Chicago Press, 1958.

E. R. Service, "Cultural Evolution." In *International Encyclopedia of the Social Sciences.* Macmillan and The Free Press, 1968, V:221–227.

E. Shils, *Center and Periphery.* University of Chicago Press, 1975.

M. Singer, *When A Great Tradition Modernizes.* Praeger, 1972.

N. J. Smelser, *Social Change in the Industrial Revolution.* University of Chicago Press, 1959.

N. J. Smelser, ed., *Sociology.* Wiley, 1973.

A. Smith, *Lectures on Justice, Police, Revenue and Arms.* Oxford: Clarendon Press, 1896.

A. Smith, *The Wealth of Nations.* Modern Library, 1937.

A. D. Smith, *The Concept of Social Change.* London: Routledge and Kegan Paul, 1973.

P. A. Sorokin, *Social and Cultural Dynamics*, 4 vols. Bedminster Press, 1962.

P. A. Sorokin, "Comments on Schneider's Criticisms." In G. K. Zollschan and W. Hirsch, eds., *Explorations in Social Change*. Houghton Mifflin, 1964, pp. 401–431.

H. Spencer, *Principles of Sociology*. Appleton. Vol. I, 1899. Vol. II, 1898. Vol. III, 1899.

H. Spencer, *The Study of Sociology*. Appleton, 1924.

H. Spencer, *First Principles*. DeWitt Revolving Fund, 1958.

O. Spengler, *The Decline of the West,* 2 vols. Knopf, 1939.

W. Stark, "Herbert Spencer's Three Sociologies." *American Sociological Review,* 1961, 26:515–521.

W. Stark, *The Sociology of Religion*, vol. IV. Fordham University Press, 1970.

W. G. Sumner, "The Absurd Effort to Make the World Over." In A. G. Keller and M. R. Davie, eds., *Essays of William Graham Sumner*, vol. I. Yale University Press, 1934.

E. P. Thompson, *The Making of the English Working Class*. Pantheon, 1964.

F. Toennies, *Fundamental Concepts of Sociology*. American Book Company, 1940.

A. J. Toynbee, *A Study of History*, vol. IV. London: Oxford University Press, 1939.

L. Trotsky, *History of the Russian Revolution*, vol. I. Simon and Schuster, 1932.

B. S. Turner, *Weber and Islam.* London: Routledge and Kegan Paul, 1974.

T. B. Veblen, *Imperial Germany and the Industrial Revolution.* Viking, 1939.

L. F. Ward, *Pure Sociology.* Macmillan, 1903.

M. Weber, *The Protestant Ethic and the Spirit of Capitalism.* London: Allen and Unwin, 1930.

M. Weber, *The Religion of China.* The Free Press, 1951.

M. Weber, *Ancient Judaism.* The Free Press, 1952.

M. Weber, *The Religion of India.* The Free Press, 1958.

M. Weber, *Gesammelte Aufsätze zur Wissenschaftslehre.* Tübingen: J. C. B. Mohr (Paul Siebeck), 1968a.

M. Weber, *Economy and Society,* 3 vols. Ed. by G. Roth and C. Wittich. Bedminster Press, 1968b.

E. Wilson, *To the Finland Station.* Harcourt, Brace, 1940.

Index

Ferguson, A., 12, 17–20, 21, 23
Forbes, D., 18
Foxes and lions, 67–70
Frazer, J. G., 3, 4, 5, 26

Gerschenkron, A., 47
Giddens, A., 84
Ginsberg, M., 15, 35, 52
Glock, C. Y., 92
Goldenweiser, A. A., 34–35
Greeley, A. M., 60
Group persistences, 67

Hammond, P. E., 92
Heard, G., 47–48
Hindu ethic, 96
Hitler, A., 71
Hobhouse, L. T., 10–12, 15,
    35, 49–54, 90–91
Hobsbawm, E. J., 83
Homogeneity and hetero-
    geneity, 5–9

Immanent change, 75–76
Industrial reserve army, 84
Industrial revolution, 7–9
Instinct for combinations, 67
Integration, 7–10

Kluckhohn, C., 113
Kroeber, A. L., 81, 105,
    109–113

Labor power, 83–84
Law of combined development,
    46–47
Lehmann, W. C., 17, 18
Lenski, G., 15
Lenski, J., 15

Lopreato, J., 66
Lukes, S., 60

McClelland, D. C., 96
MacIntyre, A., 97
Magic, 3–4
Maine, H. S., 44
Mandelbaum, M., 34
Marx, K., 23, 32–33, 55,
    80–91, 97, 101–102, 105
Meisel, J. H., 71
Merton, R. K., 60, 79, 108
Millar, J., 12, 20–23
Modern capitalism, 82–83, 92
Modernization, 95–96
Morgan, L. H., 12, 16, 18,
    30–36
Munro, T., 10
Mussolini, B., 71

Nelson, B., 92
Nisbet, R. A., 34

Ogburn, W. F., 105–109

Pareto, V., 55, 63–72, 82, 97
Parsons, T., 7, 61, 64
Penalty of taking the lead,
    45–48
Popper, K. R., 86–89
Principle of limit, 75–76
Protestant ethic, 91–98

Railway gauges, 45–46
Reason
    and change, 86–91
    and evolution, 20–22, 48–49,
        54

1 2 3 4 5 6 7 8 9–RJC–82 81 80 79 78 77 76